WHAT'S RIGHT

8 Fundamental Steps of Betterment
For Consumer Connections...
...Leading to Inevitable Success!

Written by Patrick D. St. John

Copyright © 2024 by Patrick D. St. John

All rights reserved. No part of this publication may be reproduced, distributed, or transmitted in any form or by any means, including photocopying, recording, or other electronic or mechanical methods, or conveyed via the internet or a website without the prior written permission of the author. All rights inquiries should be directed to patst.john7707@gmail.com

Registration Number

TX 9-424-931

Dedication

I would like to dedicate this project to my late father who was a proud honorably discharged World War II Marine Corp. Veteran, and by and through his disciplinary directives and Heart of gold, I have become the man I am today! Thanks Dad!

Acknowledgement

There are many contributors to this work who merit acknowledgement and heartfelt appreciation…family, friends, colleagues, mentors and yes, many consumers! The greatest of all is our creator, who has not only been a contributor to this compilation but has also been a contributor through my whole life with many opened doors of opportunities and blessings! Putting me in front of the Right people at the Right time, and the Right place at the Right time! Creating many Opportunities for Success and the ability to share the experiences that I have so graciously been given, as well as the ability to learn and grow from these experiences to enhance my value for Right Reason by being conscientious to do What's Right in all that I do! Thank You God!

About the Author

A Certified Chef by trade graduating from Scottsdale Culinary Institute. Retail Sales/Business Management by profession after graduating from Southwest Business College. Establishing over 40 years of proven people Relations and Communication Skills. Entailing 15 years in the Auto Sales Industry, over 10 years in the retail Furniture Industry, 8 years in the Radio Industry, sales and On-Air Broadcasting and Commercial Production. Over 7 years Restaurant Ownership. Now semi-retired.

Totaling over 25 years in Retail Sales and Business Management experience, involving tutoring and training of hundreds of want to be salesmen/women. Some passionate and some not so passionate. Without "passion', one cannot be self-motivated to the extent of complete success!

It is with these acquired successful experiences and unique people skills that enabled Patrick to reach a level of becoming a mentor in the public relations industry ('people business')! So much so that many of Patrick's trainees and colleagues were in appreciation of the directives, that they were motivated enough to inspire Patrick to write a training manual. It is with that encouragement and appreciation that Patrick decided that it was time to share this proven method of Betterment to a vaster audience by creating a very easy to follow step by step tutorial of simply doing "What's Right"! "Leading to a Trail of Inevitable Success"!

What's Right

A "Science", But Not a "Rocket Science" to "Customer Relationships"…

Where Objectives Are Inevitably Accomplished!

Preface

There are (**6**) six main ingredients that must be incorporated into the "Winning Recipe of Success", e.g.… **'Structure', 'Process', 'Management', 'Passion', 'Motivation',** and **"Action"**! When you add <u>YOU</u> to the mix, YOU then have **"Personal Responsibility"**, which <u>leads</u> to **"Self-Conscientiousness"**. Now, **Action** needs to be taken, with a **"PLAN"**!

Taking *'action'* requires self-***motivation***, which is relatively simple if one is *'passionate'* about their objective/objectives that <u>will</u> be ***accomplished***!

As we have all learned in life, it is full of **CHOICES** to make, and once we make a ***choice*** and decide to move forward with that ***choice*** (***taking action***), it now becomes another ***choice*** one has to make of how we decide (*choose*) to navigate the ***"original choice"***. Now you segue into a ***"process"***, but way too often the ***process*** itself is askew, and then

"wrong reason" (*motive*) kicks in and turns into reasons (*excuses*). It actually becomes a much simpler *process* toward the direction of doing *"What's Right"*! When *"Right Reason"* is the actual focus, it makes the element of *"success"* not only easier to achieve, but most importantly it makes one more *appreciative* of the accomplishment, and this my friend, includes YOU, unless one allows the "ego" to get involved. Then *choices* get muddled by a misperception in one's self where the focus is then mirrored toward one's self, where *"wrong reason"* actually becomes the starting point, which then the *"Retention Process"* is off to a bad commencement, which leads to a failed conclusion. What YOU will soon learn from this *"Betterment Process"* of DOING *"What's Right"*, is that it's not only in YOU, but it is also a responsibility and commitment when YOU choose to meet up with someone who is considered a *prospect/opportunity,* and soon to be a *"Customer"* **(Buyer/Owner)**!

The *"What's Right"* process **Never Ends!!!**

So, what does this all mean? It's **ALL** about *"The Customer"*, and it *starts* with **"YOU"**!

...Your **A**wareness, your **A**ttitude, your **A**cceptance, and taking **A**ction...

Strive for "Straight **A**'s, and do **what really makes sense**!

REFLECTIONS OF GREATNESS

OBJECTS IN THE MIRROR
USUALLY APPEAR
SMALLER THAN THEY ARE

BUT WHEN YOU LOOK IN THE MIRROR
THERE'S NO REASON TO FEAR
BECAUSE YOUR GREATNESS IS NOT THAT FAR

WHEN "YOU" LOOK IN THE MIRROR
YOU CHOOSE WHO YOU SEE
AND IT'S "YOU" THAT CHOOSES YOUR DESTINY

TO BE A MOUNTAIN
OR MERELY A MAN

TO DO "WHAT'S RIGHT"
IN ALL THAT "YOU" PLAN

WHEN "YOU" CHOOSE WHERE TO GO
IS IT HONEST & TRUE OR FULL EGO

AND WHEN YOU LOOK AT OTHERS
WHO WILL YOU SEE?

SOMEONE YOU CAN USE?
OR ALL THAT THEY CAN BE?

SO WHEN YOU SEE REFLECTIONS IN THE MIRROR
WHO DO "YOU" REALLY SEE
IS IT TRULY ABOUT OTHERS
OR IS IT ABOUT ME, ME, ME?

By Patrick St. John

3rd. or 4th. Dimension of Living?

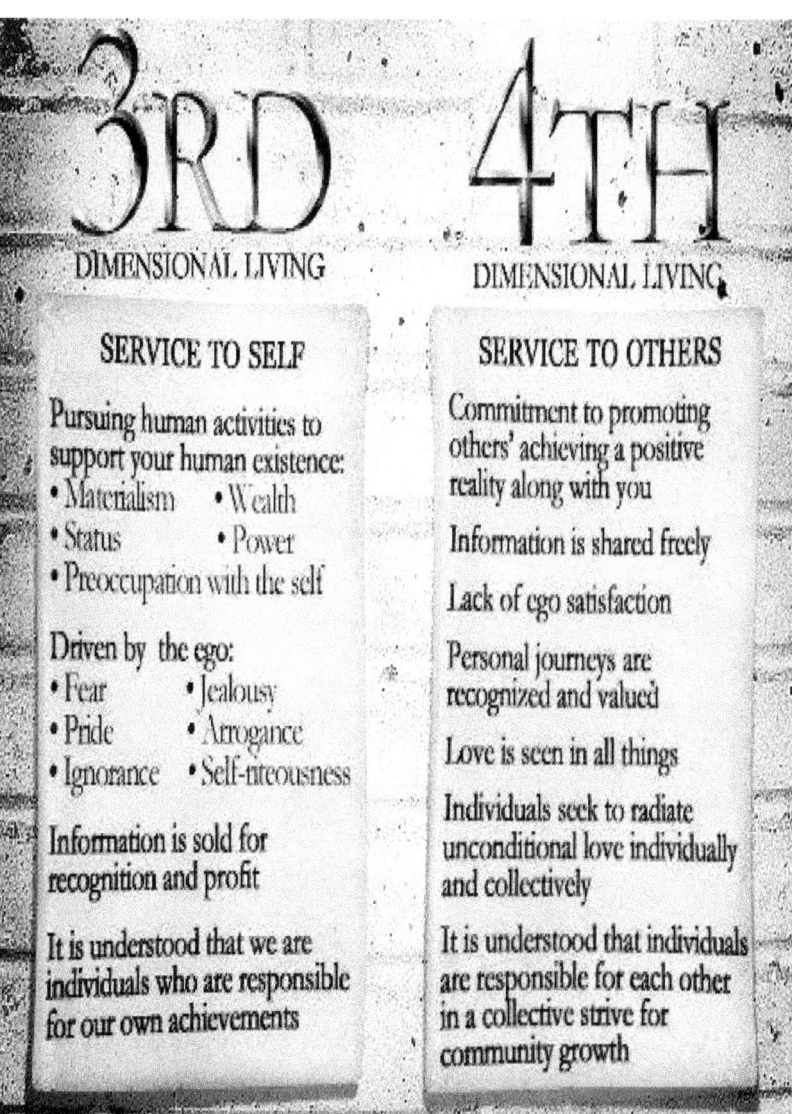

Table Of Contents

DEDICATION III
ACKNOWLEDGEMENT IV
ABOUT THE AUTHOR V
PREFACE VI
REFLECTIONS OF GREATNESS VIII
PRIMARY INTRODUCTION 1
    "What Makes Sense?" 2
    "What's Right"? 2
    The 6TH. "Sense" 4
    "The Betterment Process" 8
    "What's in a Word?" 9
    "The Hot Spot" 13
    101 Words of Relevance for a Betterment Process of doing "What's Right"… 16
    "Self-Assurance" 24
    "Psycho Cybernetics" 25
    "Affirmation Statement" 28

PROCEDURE 1 CUSTOMER RELATIONS & RELATIONSHIPS 32
    What is "Reason"? 34
    "Public Relations" 35
    "Customer Service" 36
    "Complete Satisfaction" 39
    "Integral Connections"!!! 41
    Integral Connections 43

PROCEDURE 2 THE CUSTOMER 44
    "Who Truly is #1?" 45
    "Who is a "Customer"? 46
    "Objectives" 52
    "Accomplished Automatically/Inevitably"! 53

"The Customer's Perspective"	56
"Reputation"	57
"Company's Reputation"!	59

PROCEDURE 3 GREET & MEET 61

"The Origin of the Handshake"	62
What's in a Handshake?	63
"The Handshake"!	64
"The Positive Reception Handshake"!	67
"Awareness"	69
"The Customer" is always first!	70
"Opportunity"	75
"Their Space"	78
"Connection"	79
… "The First Impression"!	79
"Mirroring"	81
"What's in a Name?"	82
"Benefit"	84
"Eye Contact"	85
"Touch"	86

PROCEDURE 4 FACT FINDING 88

"What's Right" For "The Customer".	89
"Ego"	92
"Be a Detective"	94
Not closure!	95
"Hot Buttons"	95
"Always Be Closing"!	98

PROCEDURE 5 LANDING AND COMMITTING 99

"Landing Effectively"	105
"Loyalty and Retained Business"!	107
"Emotionally Connected"!	113
"Complete Satisfaction!"	113

PROCEDURE 6 PRESENTATION & DEMONSTRATION 115

"Close the Deal with 100% Complete Satisfaction"!	118
"What's Right"!	119
"Complete Satisfaction!"	119

"Simple Science" 120
"The Presentation" 121
"Hot Buttons" 122
"Ownership Decision Awareness"! 122
"Customer Involvement" 124
"Continued Involvement" 124
"The Demonstration" 126
"Decision making/ownership process"! 128
"Panoramic Commitment of Product Knowledge"! 130

PROCEDURE 7 "MAKING IT HAPPEN" 133

"There really is no need to go to the competition!" 140
"Path of Ownership" 147

PROCEDURE 8 "BRANDING THE BRAIN" AND "THE 7 R'S" .. 149

"Achieving Your Objectives Inevitably"! 150
The 7 R's have been created to do just that…" make a mark"
…and YOU are that "MARK"! 155
Time for a referral… 161
"100% Completely Satisfied" 162

EPILOGUE 166

What's Right
*Doing it For "The Opportunity"!
Not to, "The Opportunity"*

Primary Introduction

"What Makes Sense?"

Everyone wants, and some need to <u>achieve</u> their *"Objectives"* for one reason or another, and at the same time it seems that most do it the hard way or aren't even able to pull off the task at all, some just miss the mark completely. Everyone in the business of earning "their" <u>worth</u> (commission) takes on the responsibility to depend on himself or herself to earn an honest living. When *"objectives"* are not achieved there are usually many disappointed people, all wondering what went wrong, when everything seemed to be so *"right"!* It makes no *'sense'* …Well, *"**What Makes Sense**"?*

There is a simple *"solution",* and believe me, it is <u>NOT</u> *"Rocket Science".*

It is reaching way down and asking yourself…

"What's Right"?

Stop for a moment, and think about the question… *what makes sense?* We all have *obligations*, which lead to *priorities*. What one must do is *prioritize* those <u>obligations</u> in thought, now YOU have a *'Thought Process'*, which segues into an *'obligatory thought'*. What one must do is break it down to the ridiculous, by asking yourself, ***"what's right"***? By stopping and taking the time to actually figure it all out.

YOU not only have to <u>commit</u> to those *priorities*, but YOU actually have to be somewhat of a self-detective and be *analytical* to be *effective* in routing **yourself**, and NOT subjecting yourself to, what some call normal *"rhetoric"*. Which is transitioned into *"thought patterns"*, and these patterns can actually be directed by this *rhetoric*. All one has to simply do, is *"take the bull by the horn"* and <u>lead</u> by your *"own"* <u>convictions</u>, and not by others, especially when YOU have <u>committed</u> yourself to, and in a *'Professional Position'* to be a <u>Leader</u>, not to mention YOU <u>owe</u> yourself that much *respect,* I'm sure! For then, YOU would not be abiding by other's convictions, and therefore being a leader, and not a follower. But of more *evidence,* one owes the individual in front of them, that "authentic *respect",* being that YOU depend on these individuals ("Potential Buyers") every day to earn "**their**" *worth/value*! That's *"Right"* ***their worth…*** It is <u>their</u> worth that establishes your *worth/value* and excels YOU into the elements of ***SUCCESS!!!***

Now, take another moment and ask yourself…What is actually the question of relevance here? There seems to be so many questions taking place, or are they merely questions that simply answer themselves? ***"What makes sense"*** is <u>doing</u> ***"What's Right"*** for the ***"Right Reason".*** This eliminates a question of ***"What's Right?"*** and also answers the question of ***"what makes sense"*** ("Right ***Reason***"), and at the same time, explains *"the science"* behind this <u>**"Betterment** Process"</u>!

The 6th. "Sense"

We have ALL been given the same *'gifts'* but with different traits, yet with the same *capabilities*, and those gifts are *"The 5 Senses"*. I'm confident to believe that I do not need to educate anyone on the *5 senses*…what they are, how they function, etc., but I can assist you with a better understanding of why these miraculous *"senses"* have been bestowed upon us. To strengthen our *'accomplishing capabilities'*, which requires **awareness**. When your senses are *"fully aware"*, YOU will have both **"eyes"** open paying attention to certain *"satisfaction/ownership traits"* that will be more evident when one actually *focuses* visually (*using peripheral vision at all times*); **"Listen"** *attentively* with both **ears**, actually hearing what is being said, by *"hearing between the lines"* so to speak. With this *astuteness* YOU will be more aware of *"buying/ownership signals"*; **"Speak"** only when it is *relevant* to the situation at hand, whether YOU are stating a fact, or asking questions. Ensure that your questions are not only relevant to the scenario at hand, but also *"open-ended"*, giving your soon to be owner a chance to *elaborate* and indirectly *"tie themselves down"* by revealing personal *interests* and or **concerns**. Which can be *construed* as '***mini reasons***' to accept **ownership** or to be **satisfied** with the situation that may be taking place! Use it to your *advantage* to **listen twice as much as You speak**…This is why we have been given 2 ears and one mouth…to listen twice as much as we speak. **"Touch"**; let's take the *sense* of ***touch*** to another level…How about ***feelings***…to feel is to touch things,

"*Righ*t"? So, let's go there…*to touch things Right*, YOU have to actually *feel* things *"Right"*. It's called *"Emotional Feelings"* or *involvement*. Once your *feelings* are involved, the *"6th sense"* kicks in…ESP.

"*Extra Sensory Perception*". We have all heard of it, and we ALL have it! Let's break it down…First of all, let's clarify that it's NOT in the mind, although it does travel to the mind where it branches off into the gifted *"5 senses"*.

Now let's discuss *'extra sensory perception'* by breaking it down word by word…To **perceive** is to *'recognize'* or *'feel'*; **Sensory** is a derivative of *"sense"*, and having **sense** is having *'wisdom'* or *'intellect,* and even *'feeling'*. This is where we get the term…

"Common Sense".

I was going to discuss **"common sense"** later in this write, but since we're on the subject…what is *"common sense"*, or at least how is it that this term has gotten so mixed-up in commonality, whereas most people in the profession of *"Customer Relations"*, *"miss the mark"* by not truly being aware of what a *"Consumer/Opportunity"* actually wants, and how they expect to be treated under any circumstances. Now where is the *"sense"* in that commonality? Think about it!

…Now back to the definitive term of "ESP*"*. Lastly, we have the word **extra**, pretty simple word, right? Well, the **6th sense** is not extra, "it's in there"; along with the other

"Gifted Senses", and it's to our advantage, to take advantage of these gifted *senses,* especially in the… *"Customer Relations" Profession* where it is not only a responsibility to *maintain/retain* a "Customer", but just as relevant, with Complete Satisfaction to the point of spreading the word, creating a *"referral process"* …*Retain & Refer* (R&R)

Here's the other *"miraculous gift"* (**6Th Sense**) that we have all been blessed with; and that is *"HEART"*. You've heard the term; *Have a little heart"!* Well surprise!

"We all have it" … **"Heart"!**

"HEART"

This is where most *"miss the mark"*. Not by anyone's fault but their own. It certainly was not by the *"Giver of the gifts"*. One thing that we all have *in- common* is *"The Freedom of Choice"*. In our society we have been *processed* to use only our *"senses"*, but with **"no heart"**, and that my friend, makes no *sense*. So, what's the *solution*?

"Come to your senses" and **"have heart"**, not only in your career, but also in all that you do. The *"pay off"* (objectives) is much easier to *achieve* than one might truly *comprehend*. When YOU add *"heart"* to your *"Presentation/Process"*, combined with your other *"senses"*, you will not only be more **successful** in your career, but you will also find that your *"objectives"* will be more easily achieved, *personally* and *professionally*, and on a more *consistent* basis. Now who doesn't want that? This may help put things in a more

conducive *perspective*. As we grow up in life we go through a *"process of growth"*, that we call being *taught, trained*, or what we have learned.

Somewhere along this *journey/process*, people seem to have allowed themselves to be put "inside a box" of a sort. Hence the term; *"being or feeling boxed in"* or *"think outside the box"*. In order to *"think outside the box"*, one has to take themselves out of that box in order to view things from the other side. Especially when it's a *"Customer's point of view"*! To simplify it… "YOU" have to start with an *"Open Mind"* in order to **open**

***"The Box"*!**

Here's a relatively simple question for you…simple, if YOU have an **"open mind"**.

What does a *"Human Mind"* and a *"Parachute"* have in common? ...

…They both have to be *completely* open to function *accurately"*, ending in Success!

The "key" words here are **completely** and **accurately**. Although it doesn't hurt to **open** your *"heart"* as well, for YOU to **function** just the same!

Now one may have noticed that I did not include the word ***Success*** in the above-mentioned "key" words of importance. If by chance, you did notice this omittance.

…Question is, do you know why?

Success is not to be construed as merely a *'word"*, but as an **_accomplishment_** (Success)! Where accomplishments then satisfy the mind to a *"heart's content".*

Now, think about and consider this, if the *"**Heart**'* is content and the mind is satisfied,

(*A satisfied mind that derived from the heart, which originated from the mind*). Does this not establish well-being or a state of *happiness* or even *gratification*? Therefore, "***Success***" could actually be construed as a *"state of mind"* if you stop and really think about it! Just don't kid yourself, be "true" to YOU!

With over a (35) thirty-five-year career in *"People Relations"*, I have come to the conclusion that we in fact have a **6th sense**, and it is not "mind reading", it is ***"Fact Finding"*** for the ***"Right Reason"*** by utilizing our other *"senses"* from the *"**Integral Sense**"*, and that's the **"Heart"**! Doing things from the Heart will create *'right reason'*!

"The Betterment Process"

First let's discuss the term "Betterment". As defined in the "New World Dictionary of America"; *'a making or being made better'* - *'Law of Improvement that increases the value of property and is more than mere repairs'*. In other words,

it is an actual *"Change"* of something, not temporal or part-time, which increases its **value**, and that *value* is **"YOU"**!

Compiled in the forwarding text are (8) eight fundamental *procedures* of a *"Betterment Process"* which is <u>essential</u> to the *"<u>success</u>"* of any individual that is on the *path,* or is <u>committed</u> to, a <u>career</u> of <u>earning</u> their $$$ *"<u>worth</u>"* in a *"Face to Face"* or *"One-on-One"* scenario (*"Customer Relations"*). Each and every one of us has been *'gifted'* with the *'utmost potential'* to ***succeed*** and be **#1**. Equivalent to a *"Customer,* if we *'understand* 'how, and also ***choose*** to do so! Although, another question does arise and becomes somewhat of an *enigma,* or a "<u>shortfall</u>" in reaching *"The Top"*!

Who is, *"in fact* **# 1???**

This *question* is considerably easier to answer once YOU have <u>ALL</u> the **FACTS**…and it all starts in a "WORD"! Trust" me, YOU <u>will</u> be *"Self-assured"* that this *"Betterment Process"* of <u>doing</u> *"What's Right",* is *RIGHT,* and it's "**In You**"!

In a "**WORD**", with "***Action***", you <u>can</u> *"Obtain Your Objectives Inevitably!"*

"What's in a Word?

One thing I have found throughout my career in *"Human Communications",* is that many people not only misuse the "American" language, but also don't grasp their different <u>meanings</u> or *connotations.*

As we begin this **"Betterment Process"** of *"Doing <u>IT FOR</u> "The Opportunity",*

And *<u>NOT TO</u>, "The Opportunity"!*

Not only is it *imperative* to use the proper *verbiage/vocabulary* as YOU proceed to the "<u>Close</u>" (*earning one's business*), but as we *progress* along the way to doing **"What's Right"**, YOU will find many words or phrases in *"quotations"*, '*apostrophized*' and *italicized* format. These **"words"** have a *congruent,* and or **"Rational Value"** that will help you in establishing a greater <u>understanding</u>, and '<u>judicial reasoning</u>' with your *"Guest/Opportunity/Consumer"*!

As well as help YOU <u>Relate</u> to your *Guest/Opportunity* in a more *conducive* manner that will **automatically** *establish* **"RIGHT REASON"!**

"WORDS" of "Relational Relevance for a Betterment Process".

To assist in a better understanding of the <u>Words</u> of *relational relevance*, in the forwarding text is a compilation of these **essential words**…all are simple words, yet when elaborated on they become much more vast in meaning, and by following this *"informative process",*

You will find that the selected words may be simple words, although they do become more of a required directive in the *paradigm shift thought process* of doing

"*What's Right*"!

The chosen words are simply more defined so that one can have a greater understanding of the **value** of doing "*What's Right*"!

"Now, this is very ***valuable!***"

...take each word and do a more thorough Synonym/Thesaurus research. I am very confident to believe that you will not only be intrigued, but also, I hope excited to learn the "***importance***" of these words and how they ***relate*** to one another in this "*Betterment Process*". By studying and cross-referencing each word, YOU will not only *obtain* a stronger grip-hold of their meaning, but also the depth of each word and their "***integral connections***". This will also add more depth to YOU, producing more *efficiency*, and *success*, but most importantly, a "*greater perception*" of these words and how to actually get the picture and utilize them more **Effectively** and more **Lucratively!** Whether it be verbal communication or an enhanced thought process!

NOTE: The *reasoning* behind me as the writer of this text for not including a complete Synonym/Thesaurus research, is that the "*Betterment Process*" requires "*Personal involvement*"!

To fully accept the *reasoning* behind the forthcoming "words", One has to go beyond the concept of '*communication*' and **lock-in** on the concept of *connectivity*, The selected **"words"** have been chosen to not only assist

YOU with proper chosen grammar, but most importantly the *"Relational Connectivity"* and *"Relational Value"* of <u>each word</u>. For this element/ingredient of success is elementary in the *'Betterment Process'* of doing ***"What's Right."*** *"Customers/Consumers"* are not really concerned about proper grammar as much as they are concerned about <u>***proper communication***</u> with *Honest Concern,* ***"Integrity and Compassion"!***

"Take my <u>word</u> for it" that YOU will not be disappointed by *implementing* this *application.* Providing that YOU are not continuing in vain, not only in this read, but in your life's journey as well. I can also *assure* YOU, that YOU and anyone that is *connected* to *Your Objectives*, will also *ascend* closer to theirs, which can only make YOU a...

"Hero, instead of a zero"!!!

Please take note... this is not to be construed, nor is it intended to be a language lesson! Being that You are reading and continuing to follow along in this read, I am confident to believe you are fully aware of the *American language*, but do You realistically ***value*** and <u>accept</u> the *responsibility* we possess to get <u>*the whole picture*</u> **Right***?*

"A picture paints a thousand words"!

To *"get the whole picture"* **Right**...YOU must acquire an astute understanding of which *vocabulary* and or *'thought process'* YOU choose, to either *enhance* or *diminish* your

<u>forward momentum</u>! And it's a *"simple science"* if YOU work with and aim for the **"Hot Spot!"**

"The Hot Spot"

- Some say that their **"Hearts"** are for friends and family, and that their mind and muscle is for work.
- Some may even say that being "Nice" can be dangerous, i.e. *"Nice guys finish last"* … Do they really?
- Based on recent surveys compiled by HBR ("Harvard Business Review"), more workers would trust a stranger, more than they would trust their own boss.
- Actually, when we **<u>choose</u>** to leave *"Heart"* out of the scheme of things and leave the *"role"* of *'<u>emotions</u>'* behind, it stagnates **"Relational Growth**!
- People are **"Human Beings"**, not to be deemed as uncompromising icons, but as **<u>"valuable assets!</u> "**
- It is very **<u>imperative</u>** and **<u>influential</u>** to **<u>initiate</u>** **"Heart"** from **<u>"the core"</u>** of who YOU truly are, and what YOU do! When done so…

You've hit the *"**Hot Spot!!!***

To assist in hitting the "Hot Spot" it's very essential to be aware of the role of emotions, and have an astute understanding of the cognitive differences between a '*negative*' emotion and a "*positive*" emotion…

"Role of Emotions"

Negative: During stress and *'Negative Emotions'*, **"Heart"** rhythm is disordered, corresponding neural signals traveling from the <u>heart</u> to the <u>brain</u> effect higher '*cognitive functions*!

Positive: In contrast, the more ordered and stable pattern of the "Heart's" input to the brain during *"Positive Emotional States"* has the opposite effect, which facilitates cognitive function for **"Right Reason"**.

To completely understand the importance of '*Emotional Connections'*, **"Right Reason"** <u>must</u> apply! This process, again, is not a *Rocket Science*! Although a science is *necessitated*. The *"science"* of which I am referring, is so simple, for the fact, it is instilled in every one of us from the get-go. It just takes aptness to implement this *"science"*. When done so, a **"connection"** is <u>***automatically established***</u>. One simply needs to create a balance between… *"**Heart"*** and ***"Mind"!***

What is "Science"?

Subject Matter… such as to; *'educate'*, *'regulate'* or *'control'*, *to have discipline over, 'knowledge', 'skill'*, or an *'art'* of doing!

With the incorporation of this **"Simple Science"**, it will direct YOU toward a <u>vocabulary of understanding</u> for the ***"Right Reason"*** and catapult You to a much higher level of success!

Perfect segue to Words 101, a <u>vocabulary of understanding</u> of which are relevant words that are connected to the

"Betterment Process" of <u>doing</u> **"What's Right"**!

101 Words of Relevance for a Betterment Process of doing "What's Right"...

(*Right Reason!*)

Right: (adv.) accurate (adj.) respectable (adj.) moral (adj.) genuine (v.) restore (n.) entitlement

Reason: (n.) motive (v.) goal (n.) intelligence (v.) rationalize (n.) senses (v.) persuade

1. **Ability:** (*n.*) *aptitude, skill, capability, talent, gift, power, etc.*
2. **Acceptance:** (*n.*) *belief, acknowledgment, agreement, approval, concurrence, etc.*
3. **Accomplish:** (*v.*) *achieve, realize, complete, do, get done, undertake, etc.*
4. **Acknowledge:** (*v.*) *admit, greet, respond, grant, allow, accept, recognize, etc.*
5. **Action:** (*n.*) *act, accomplish, achievement, engagement, encounter, deed, stroke, etc.*
6. **Advance:** (*v.*) *proceed, progress, improve, increase,* (*n.*) *forward movement, etc,*
7. **Advantage:** (*n.*) *benefit, gain, bonus, lead, improvement, help, plus, pro, etc.*

8. **Affirmation:** (*n.*) *confirmation, assertion, verification, support, encouragement, etc.*
9. **Assist:** (*n.*) *help, aid, support, contribution, backing, promotion, etc.*
10. **Associate:** (*n.*) *connect, relate, link, unite, join together, partner, companion, ally, etc.*
11. **Attitude:** (*n.*) *approach, outlook, manner, feelings, position, mind-set, stance, etc.*
12. **Aura:** (*n.*) *air, atmosphere, feeling, impression, characteristic, quality, appearance, etc.*
13. **Authenticity:** (*n.*) *genuineness, validity, realism, dependability, accuracy, etc.*
14. **Awareness:** (*n.*) *consciousness, alertness, knowledge, grasp, appreciation, etc.*
15. **Believe:** (*v.*) *consider, think, suppose, deem, trust, accept as true, etc.*
16. **Betterment:** (*n.*) *improvement, development, progress, prosperity, promotion, etc.*
17. **Can:** (*n.*) *be capable of, know how to,* (*v.*) *preserve, maintain, continue, etc.*
18. **Care:** (*n.*) *treatment, attention, thought, consideration, precision, control, etc.*
19. **Change:** (*v.*) *transform, adjust, convert,* (*n.*) *adjustment, resolution, difference, etc.*
20. **Character:** (*n.*) *integrity, reputation, nature, personality, quality, moral fiber, spirit, etc.*
21. **Cherish:** (*v.*) *treasure, value, appreciate, esteem, prize, attach importance to, etc.*
22. **Choice:** (*n.*) *option, abundance, wealth,* (*adj.*) *high-quality, cream of the crop, etc.*
23. **Commitment:** (*n.*) *promise, obligation, dedication, loyalty, responsibility, duty, etc.*

24. **Compassion:** (*n.*) *empathy, concern, kindness, consideration, care, etc.*
25. **Complete:** (*adj.*) *absolute, inclusive, comprehensive, wide-ranging, thorough, etc.*
26. **Confidence:** (*n.*) *self-assurance, coolness, belief, trust, loyalty, certainty, assertion, etc.*
27. **Connection:** (*n.*) *link, association, relationship, relation, bond, union, etc.*
28. **Contentment:** (*n.*) *satisfaction, happiness, pleasure, gratification, ease, etc.*
29. **Control:** (*v.*) *manage, organize, direct,* (*n.*) *management, influence, self-control, etc.*
30. **Courtesy:** (*n.*) *good manners, politeness, consideration, civility, etc.*
31. **Customer:** (*n.*) *client, purchaser, buyer, patron, consumer, etc.*
32. **Decision:** (*n.*) *choice, result, resolution, determination, resolve, certitude, etc.*
33. **Desire:** (*n.*) *want, yearning, craving, need,* (*v.*) *request, require, implore, pray, etc.*
34. **Devotion:** (*n.*) *attachment, dedication, care, attentiveness, enthusiasm, etc.*
35. **Direction:** (*n.*) *route, path, objective, aim, management, leadership, etc.*
36. **Effective:** (*adj.*) *successful, useful, real, valuable, actual, operational, etc.*
37. **Empathy:** (*n.*) *understanding, sympathy, compassion, etc.*
38. **Endure:** (*v.*) *last, continue, carry on, keep on, persist, etc.*
39. **Energy:** (*n.*) *power, force, vigor, liveliness, get-up-and-go, oomph, etc.*
40. **Evolve:** (*v.*) *develop, change, grow, progress, advance, go forward, etc.*

41. **Excel:** (*v.*) *surpass, do extremely well, shine, standout, outclass, etc.*
42. **Excitement:** (*n.*) *enthusiasm, anticipation, stimulation, pleasure, thrill, etc.*
43. **Expand:** (*v.*) *get bigger, enlarge, increase, develop, spread out, etc.*
44. **Fairness:** (*n.*) *justice, equality, honesty, integrity, validity, reasonableness, etc.*
45. **Focus:** (*n.*) *center, focal point, heart, motivation, application,* (*v*) *converge, target, etc.*
46. **For:** (*prep.*) *meant for, in favor of, pro, in support of, representing, etc.*
47. **Forward:** (*adv.*) *onward,* (*v.*) *advance, promote,* (*adj.*) *presumptuous, brazen, etc.*
48. **Frequent:** (*adj.*) *recurrent, regular, normal, numerous, many, repeated, etc.*
49. **Fulfillment:** (*n*) *completion, realization, performance, satisfaction, success, joy, etc.*
50. **Gain:** (*v.*) *increase, grow, expand, achieve, win, obtain,* (*n.*) *profit, reward, improve, etc.*
51. **Generous:** (*adj.*) *giving, charitable, bighearted, kind, liberal, etc.*
52. **Goal:** (*n.*) *objective, aim, ambition, purpose, target, aspiration, etc.*
53. **Growth:** (*n.*) *increase, expansion, escalation development, progress, advance, etc.*
54. **Happiness:** (*n.*) *contentment, pleasure, joy, delight, gladness, exhilaration, etc.*
55. **Heart:** (*n.*) *compassion, empathy, feeling, kindness, concern, center, core, middle, etc.*
56. **Help:** (*n.*) *assistance, benefit, service, comfort,* (*v.*) *promote, encourage, advance, etc.*

57. **Honesty:** (*n.*) truthfulness, *sincerity, integrity, candor, openness, etc.*
58. **Honor:** (*n.*) *respect, reputation, principle, pride, privilege, award,* (*v.*) *revere, keep, etc.*
59. **Increase:**(*v.*) *multiply, intensify, escalate, build-up,* (*n.*) *upsurge, growth, spread, etc.*
60. **Inspire:** (*v.*) *motivate, encourage, instigate, enthuse, arouse, stir-up, move, etc.*
61. **Integral:** (*adj.*) *essential, important, primary, central, internal, at the heart of, etc.*
62. **Integrity:** (*n.*) *honesty, truthfulness, honor, veracity, reliability, uprightness, etc.*
63. **Involvement:** (*n.*) *participation, association, attachment, connection, enthusiasm, etc.*
64. **Justice:** (*n.*) *fairness, honesty, integrity, validity, acceptability, reasonableness, etc.*
65. **Justification:** (*n.*) *good reason, reason, explanation, validation, rationalization, etc.*
66. **Knowledge:** (*n.*) *wisdom, learning, awareness, realization, comprehension, skill, etc.*
67. **Loyal/Loyalty:** (*adj.*) *faithful, trustworthy, devoted, reliable, steadfast, constant, etc.*
68. **Maintain:** (*v.*) *retain, preserve, keep, continue, sustain, keep-up, take care of, etc.*
69. **Management:** (*n.*) *organization, supervision, administration, operation, etc.*
70. **Motivation:** (*n.*) *incentive, inspiration, enthusiasm, reason, motive, purpose, etc.*
71. **Need:** (*v.*) *require, necessitate, should,* (*n.*) *essential, prerequisite, necessary, etc.*
72. **Observe/Observation:** (*v.*) *monitor, detect, perceive, respect, conform to, keep, etc.*

73. **Open/Openness:** (*adj.*) *approachable, friendly, receptive,* (*v.*) *commence, honest, etc.*
74. **Passion:** (*n.*) *fervor, excitement, enthusiasm, zeal, craze, delight, etc.*
75. **Patience:** (*n.*) *endurance, tolerance, persistence, fortitude, lack of complaint, etc.*
76. **Perseverance:** (*n.*) *insistence, urgency, firmness, resolve, determination, etc.*
77. **Plan:** (*n.*) *strategy, map, preparation,* (*v.*) *arrange, intend, propose, mean, etc.*
78. **Positive/Positivity:** (adj.) *optimism, helpful, certain, convinced, confident, etc.*
79. **Preserve:** (*v.*) *maintain, continue, sustain, safeguard, save, care for, etc.*
80. **Process:** (*n.*) *procedure, development, progression, method, practice,* (*v.*) *manage, etc.*
81. **Progress:** (*n.*) *development, improvement, advancement,* (*v.*) *improve, increase, etc.*
82. **Promotion:** (*n.*) *encouragement, help, support, elevation, upgrade, advancement, etc.*
83. **Reality:** (*n.*) *actuality, authenticity, truth, certainty, veracity, etc.*
84. **Reason:** (*n.*) *cause, motive, motivation, incentive, aim, goal, purpose, intention, etc.*
85. **Refer/Referral:** (*n.*) *pass on, submit, recommendation, appointment, etc.*
86. **Reflection:** (*n.*) *mirror image, likeness, manifestation, consideration, contemplation, etc.*
87. **Relate:** (*v.*) *communicate, connect, link, associate, interact, form a relationship, etc.*
88. **Relationship:** (*n.*) *association, connection, affiliation, rapport, correlation, bond, etc.*

89. **Repetition:** (*n.*) *recurrence, reiteration, reappearance, etc.*
90. **Respect:** (*n.*) *esteem, respect, sense,* (*v.*) *acknowledge, appreciate, regard, accept, etc.*
91. **Retain:** (*v.*) *keep, hold on to, preserve, maintain, save, etc.*
92. **Self:** (*n.*) *personality, character, identity, etc.*
93. **Sincere/Sincerity:** (*adj.*) *genuine, honest, truthful, earnest, heartfelt, authenticity, etc.*
94. **Structure:** (*v.*) *arrange, organize, construct, put together, build-up, shape, etc.*
95. **Success:** (*n.*) *achievement, accomplishment, victory, triumph, winner, sensation, star, etc.*
96. **Tangible:** (*adj.*) *touchable, real, substantial, actual, certain, evident, definite, etc.*
97. **Trail:** (*v.*) *follow, tail, shadow,* (*n.*) *pathway, way, route, imprints, path, etc.*
98. **Transition:** (*n.*) *change, evolution, shift, switch, revision, modification, etc.*
99. **Value:** (*n.*) *importance, significance, usefulness, meaning, profit,* (*v.*) *appreciate, respect, etc.*
100. **Vision:** (*n.*) *idea, mental picture, image, farsightedness, forethought, prediction, etc.*
101. **Want:** (*v.*) *desire, would like, feel like, yearn for, be after, be looking for, require, care for, like, need, require, aspire, would like, aim, intention, plan, choose, mean, etc.*

With this compilation and synonym breakdown of these 101 relevant words for a "***Betterment Process***", it is not only my hope and desire, but most importantly my recommendation to not only be familiar with these relevant words, but also have an understanding and acceptance that these words can assist in leading You to a much simpler process in relating and communicating with your/companies' opportunity, which will segue into a stronger **'*connection*'**, enhancing your 'opportunity' to earn what and or whom it is that you are investing your time and energy <u>for</u>!

You may have noticed that the one hundred and one word (*word 101*) is 'WANT', and that it has the most *synonyms* listed. Now the question is…do you know why I chose to not only elaborate more on the word 'want', but why I also chose it to be the last word, other than it being near the end of the alphabetic form. Here is why…I first wanted you, the reader, to have the last word of which you had just read, fresh in your mind. Making it easier to recall; secondly, making it easier to segue into the significance of the word '*want*', as simple as the word may appear, to make anything happen one has to first have a keen understanding of what "want is, and then have a desire before any action can be taken!

Go figure that it that the last word is 'want' and yet it is the first thing that one must do to get anything done!

"Self-Assurance"

Now that **YOU** have informed *Yourself* that a *"Betterment Process"* is possible. I am *assured* that **YOU** are still with me, and that YOU are *"self-assured"* in the same, and I do not mean simply by reading along, but actually **getting the whole picture**! Here is more assistance on doing *"What's Right"*!

Self-Assurance is so much more than merely having a ring of *confidence* in *one's self*, although, YOU most certainly need to be *Self-Confident* to be *esteemed*, but if one digs a little deeper on the subject of **Self-Assurance**, and has a realistic understanding of the term. To have *esteem,* is to '*appreciate',* and have *value* or *worth*! YOU would then find that to be <u>assured</u>, or to have <u>assurance</u>, is much more than just being poised or having a strong belief in one's self. YOU have to actually <u>assert</u> Yourself with a <u>guarantee</u> that YOU in **Fact** will **Succeed** in *accomplishing* your *objectives*. It is a much simpler process when something, or YOU is based on <u>FACT</u> …Well, here <u>YOU</u> are, and here <u>It</u> is…A **"Betterment Process"** that works, if YOU **choose** and <u>possess</u> the *"SELF-ASSURANCE"* to do
"WHAT'S RIGHT In You"!

At the beginning of my sales career, one of the studies I was involved in, and was highly intrigued by…which upon its introduction to me, the thought was a merely a concept, once implemented, I factually found that it's actually a **"science"**, and a simple one at that, penned as *"Psycho Cybernetics"*.

"Psycho Cybernetics"

"psycho", is a root word referring to the *"Mental Process"* related to the *mind,* defined as (Psyche) *'Consciousness', 'Awareness'*, i.e. *'Breath', 'Spirit', 'Soul'; a combining form* of the *mind or mental* process…*"Cybernetics"…Was coined in 1948 by Norbert Weiner,* and defined as… *'Helmsman', to steer or govern; the science dealing with the comparative study of "Human Control" systems, as the brain and nervous system….* To simplify it in layman terms, **_mind guiding_** or **_choice_ making**...It's entirely up to **"YOU"**, to

"Make it Happen"!!!

"YOU"

What a great topic, "YOU"! Speaking of which, I'm confident to believe that since YOU have come thus far, that YOU want to *Get it Right*, although I am curious what it was that directed YOU to this book in reference to what is *positioned* on the front cover… Stop and ask Yourself… was it the title? *"What's Right"*, was it…

"Doing it For "The Opportunity", "Not to "The Opportunity"!

"The Handshake", or a <u>Fact</u> that YOU <u>can</u> and <u>WILL</u> *attain* a…

"Betterment Process" to success…if <u>YOU</u> Choose!

For a greater understanding of *"Mind Guiding"* and *"Thought Patterns"*, and how to manage and direct yourself to success in everything that YOU do…I highly recommend for YOU to invest in the book *"Psycho Cybernetics"*, authored by Maxwell Maltz in 1960. Or another topical book co-authored by Charles Schreiber; *"How to Live and Be Free"* through *"Psycho Cybernetics"*, written in 1975. I assure YOU; these recommended books will factually strengthen and enhance your abilities for success if <u>YOU</u> <u>choose</u> to do so, and it all starts with <u>YOU</u> and *"Goals"*!

"Goals"

Everyone, at one time or another will come to their *Senses* and search out ways to improve themselves or whatever it is that they may do for a living…It's actually rather *simple*…All YOU need to do is <u>accentuate</u> *Honesty, Self-awareness* and *Self-motivation*, which creates, *Self-Acceptance*. Set *"Realistic Goals"* <u>in writing</u>, otherwise the goal is merely an idea, and not set in stone to yourself. <u>Goals</u> are <u>*commitments*</u> to yourself, and *"Strategic Plan"* (<u>realistic</u> plan), and then *Self-motivate*! In a nutshell…All one has to do is simply *restore* their <u>own</u> *intellect*, and direct themselves toward doing *"What's Right!"*

Here's a suggestion for YOU in reference to *"Goal Achievement"* and *"Accomplishing Your Objectives Automatically/Inevitability"!* As I previously mentioned about having *"Realistic Sound Goals"* in <u>writing</u>…YOU can simplify the process of *"goal achievement"*, by signifying

whatever it is that YOU have determined as your *Top Priority* or *Objective*, then break it down from there…to the ridiculous!

If your main *objective* is numerical, write that number down on several pieces of paper, ("Stick-ems" work best) and stick them wherever it is that YOU are on a *consistent* or daily basis…such as your morning mirror, on your car dashboard, in your office, etc. This actually is a form of *"self-brainwashing"*, or *'self-convincing'*. Also known as an *affirmation* to YOURSELF, and if YOU are at least *committed* to YOU, and *cognitive* enough to grasp what this *process* of doing *"What's Right"* can realistically do for YOU in succeeding, not only in your *'primary objective'*, but actually catapult YOU into another dimension of *success*, i.e. "Top Gun"; *winnings, volume sales, gross profit, recognition,* and a **Bigger Paycheck!!!**

With *"bigger paychecks"*, it's not rocket *science*, *Bigger Objectives* and *Goals* can be achieved. Just stay focused on doing **"What's Right"**. Taking each step (*Procedures* and *Objectives*) one step at a time for what morally makes *sense,* and I don't mean *what makes sense* just in the moment, but for the long haul (the BIG Picture). Take a few steps back, getting out of that **box** that may prevent YOU from achieving the ***true success*** that **YOU** truly *desire* and *deserve!!!*

Here is another proven *fact* when *setting Goals*. To *transition* Your *Goal* from *thought* into *reality*, establish a *focus* just beyond your main *"Aspired Target"*, i.e. ***"Goal Objective"*!**

Here's an example…While studying the martial arts in my mid-teens, the first thing that was established to the class by my "Sensei" (instructor), was learning the *"process meaning"* of the *art's* profoundness. It was instructed by the Sensei and defined as, "Putting yourself in a state of *relaxation* and *calm,* **connecting** with one's **_Inner self_**, but most importantly, staying focused on your subject's entirety; (the *Consumer/Opportunity* and the *Company* YOU work with), **focusing** just beyond or through your **target** (goal). All the while, being fully aware of your surroundings entirely. Of course, there are many other *intricacies* to the art of martial arts, but that is not what is of topic here. The point is this, stay *cool, calm, collected,* and **focused** just beyond your *target* (main objective), to attain the original *goal,* and then some! Now, **AFFIRM** it to yourself in writing *("Righting")*!!!

"Affirmation Statement"

Here's another ingredient to make it a little easier for YOU in *'achieving your objectives'*. It's called an **"affirmation statement"**! This is a *"Statement" of Confirmation"* to yourself verifying as fact, that You have arrived, or in NOW!
Whatever it is that motivates You, whether it is financial reward or something materialistically tangible. Write whatever it is, confirming as fact, in the now…here's an example……*It is a beautiful sunny day on this 10th day of June, 2022 @ 2:34 pm; and I am driving across country in my new 'Corvette' heading to 'San Diego' to close on my 'Beach-front Property' located in the suburb of 'La Jolla'*

What is being implied here are several *goals* and or *objectives*, a *New Corvette, Driving Cross Country, Going to San Diego, Purchasing Beach-front Property in La Jolla.* An *"affirmation statement"* does not have to be this elaborate, it just must be <u>honest, realistic,</u> and something that is fitting to **YOU!**

Let's define **"affirm"**; (v.) *'assert', 'insist' 'establish', 'verify'.* (n.) *'sustain'.*

An *"Affirmation"* is to <u>assert</u> to one's self, and <u>insist</u> on <u>establishing,</u> a realistic **achievement** with <u>verification</u> and <u>sustaining</u> it!

OK, I know you're ready to" Close" the next deal and prevail on getting the ball rolling toward your career in **"Customer Relationships"**, by implementing this

"Betterment Process" to doing **"What's Right"** for <u>***Inevitable Success***</u>!!!

As You have been reading and following along thus far, it is my hope that you are not reluctant in implementing this *"Betterment Process to Success"* in all that YOU do! When I state, "Inevitable Success", or "Achieving Your Objectives Automatically", it is not something to be taken with a grain of salt, for this **Process** is not a hypothesis, but years of *"proven fact"*!

When One, truly **"Cares"** about others, it is a *"Continuous Circle"* of

<u>***Inevitable Success***</u>!!!

What's Right

Doing it For... *"The Opportunity"*!
Not to... *"The Opportunity"*!

Procedure 1
Customer Relations & Relationships
Customer-Care

Procedure 2
"The Customer"
Who Really Matters

Procedure 3
Greet & Meet
"The Customer"
Awareness and Relationship Creation

Procedure 4
Fact Finding for
"The Customer"
Relationship Building

Procedure 5
Landing and Committing
"The Customer"
Benefits

Procedure 6
Presentation & Demonstration for
"The Customer"
Benefits

Procedure 7
Tie Downs & Making it Happen! for
"The Customer"
Closing the Deal

Procedure 8
Branding The Brain
&
The 7 R's
*Responsibility, Respect, Rapport, Reputation,
Relationship, Retain, Refer*
"It is YOU that they will REMEMBER!"

What's Right
Doing it For "The Opportunity"!
Not to, "The Opportunity"

Procedure 1
Customer Relations
& Relationships

Procedure 1 — Customer Relations & Relationships

In the process of establishing *"Customer Relationships"* and retaining them with the hopes of referrals, it all begins with *"Consumer Affairs"* which has many facets. Anyone individual that is in the profession of sales knows what a *"Consumer"* is, but let's take moment and expand on the word '*Affair*'...I'll start with a noun, e.g. (*n.*) '*matter*', and now a verb for '*matter*', e.g. (*v.*) '*count*', *be of importance*', '*be significant*', '*carry some weight*', '*make a difference*', '*have a bearing*', be relevant, etc.

Now does it really '*matter*' if YOU do *"What's Right"* when dealing with '*Consumers/Customers/People*'? The answer should be an aphetic "YES" if You want to first earn their business (*get their money that they work so hard for just as You and I*). **YES,** it really does *Matter* in the Relationship building process! Let's not forget, it's not a one- shot deal... referrals, referrals, referrals!!!

Here are the six (6) vital elements (*ingredients*) in the equation of *"Consumer Affairs"* and *"Customer Relationships;* '*Public Relations*', '*Customer Service*', '*Customer Care*' '*Customer Satisfaction*', '*Customer Retention*'**, and** '*Customer Referrals*'...With the completion of these 6 '*fundamental elements*', the equation is evident that **"*Customer Care*"** leads the pack!

Take the A out of the word CARE and replace it with the letter O... you now have "CORE"!

To fully <u>understand</u> the term *"Customer Care"*, you have to start by comprehending the true meaning of *"Relation/Relations"*, and its importance...first, in order to have *"relations"*, one has to be skilled in relating to people with <u>sincere</u> and <u>compassionate</u> **actions**, not only in your demeanor, but actually... **CARING** about *"Customer's"* **concerns** and or **interests**, from the "CORE" of one's self with *validity and "Reason"*!

33

What is "Reason"?

As defined in Merriam-Webster Dictionary...

(n): a statement offered in explanation or justification, (n): a rational ground or motive (reason to act promptly); (n): the/a thing that makes fact intelligible; (n): the power of comprehending, inferring, or thinking, especially in orderly rational ways (intelligence).

(v): take part in conversation or discussion; (v): to talk with another so as to influence action or opinion. Transitive verb: to justify or support with 'reasons'; to persuade or influence by the use of 'reason'; to discover, formulate, or conclude by the use of 'reason'.

"Relations" even include (n) family members, relatives, dealings, associations, interactions, affairs, contacts, and "Relationships".

By looking and now having a full comprehension of the definitive terms of Relation/Relations, even with family member and relatives in the mix, would one want to ever not get it **"Right"**?

Here's the missing ingredient to the antidote for a long termed "**Relation**", and that is, "SHIP"! That's "Right", it's as simple as that...add ship to relation and you have the perfect connection for a "RELATIONSHIP"! Just make sure that when YOU add the "SHIP" to **relation**, that it is not the "Titanic'! Make proper connections for **"Right Reason"** to ensure the true meaning of "CARE"!

Now let's make a **"Care Connection"**; (n.) 'attentiveness', 'precision', 'consideration', 'thoughtfulness', 'guidance', 'supervision'; (v.) 'concern', 'interest', etc.

With this "**Care Connection**" YOU should have a better grasp and **"Relation"** to the term!

Procedure 1 — Customer Relations & Relationships

"**Relation**" is the way in which two or more concepts, objects, or <u>people</u> are connected; a thing's effect on, or relevance to another! The way in which two or more people feel and behave toward each other!

For the sake of staying on subject of **"Relationships"** let's add 'people' to the equation...

"Public Relations"

"Public Relations" is very similar to *"Customer Service"*, a <u>connection</u> must be established, or an <u>association</u> if you will, but on a much larger scale. *"Public Relations"* has more to do with *"Company Positioning"* in the marketplace, although it does begin with *"Customer Service"*. An impression is perceived by any one individual, and **"word-of-mouth"** begins, and an image, or opinion that is created (*Reputation*). Knowing how to communicate the *"Company's Position"* helps relate to and with the "public" on a *"personal level"*. This <u>principle</u> is crucial to any *"service"* oriented business, for without the **"public"** an *association* and or a <u>relationship</u> cannot be established, therefore the <u>objective</u> of **"Complete Satisfaction"** is negated, and other *goals* and *objectives* also will not be achieved! Another important element to *"Public Relations"* and a fact that exists, is there are two sides to every coin, and one of those sides of the coin is how well *"The Company"* implements and enforces *"Company Policy"*, as well as how well *"The Company"* cares for their employees, and how well *"The Employees"* enjoy being part of the organization. When a person feels like a participant rather than merely a pawn, their <u>attitude</u> and <u>aura</u>, as well as <u>*"enthusiastic participation"*</u>, is enhanced to the utmost degree, and a natural *"positive nature"* is perceived. The bottom line is this..." The Golden Rule" applies... *"Treat People as "YOU" would like to be Treated"!*

This rule has to be applied from the very beginning of the *"Relationship Building Process"*, for it is well known that there are no second chances on *"first impressions"*. If a *"positive impression"* has not been established from the beginning, it will make it harder to acquire a *"Customer"*, let alone retain them!

"Customer Service"

Many businesses use the term *"Customer Service"* when taking care of their *"Customers"*, where this is actually an incorrect term when catering to a *"Customer"*, for the fact that *"Customers"* normally do not need to be serviced, although they do need to be taken **"CARE"** of. Here's the dilemma…Being that" Customers" always need to be *"taken care of"*, it needs to take place from the very beginning of the *"Customer Relations/Relationship"* process and be instilled with the attitude as a *never-ending process!*

A company does not need to be in the retail commodity business, such as "Wal-Mart" or "Home Depot" and such, in order to understand and implement the actual purpose of this "service"!

Let's discuss the term "SERVICE"; to **"serve"** is to *examine* the situation and *assist* in the ***BEST WAY*** possible, even if a *sacrament* or *reparation* must be made. Another facet to **"service"** is *performance*, which then segues into *"serving"*, and when one is **"serving"**, they now work for that individual toward the direction of ***"Complete Satisfaction"***, to ALL parties involved, and that includes YOU!

Even if YOU are in a profession of being a waiter or a waitress, the term is "server". These *"servers"* devote themselves to the ones they are *serving* (*"The "Customer/Guests"*), hoping to *"earn their worth"*, and their own, even to the extent of being treated rudely and or unappreciated. Go figure. This is when the "guests" themselves, are they *really* being **"served"**, or are they? One of two things are being insinuated in this type of scenario...as the above mentions...One, the "guests" are not truly being served, or at least not to **"their satisfaction"**, or two, the *"communication"* and *"actions"* are not in check...Think about it! In other words, a *"Guest/Consumer"* will not normally be a stick in the mud so to speak, unless they have just cause or are merely on the defense due to previous experiences. This is where YOU come in as an *'astute professional'* and break the ice with honed awareness and grand personality knowing that your main objective is to ensure *'Complete Service Satisfaction'* for your **guest**, the **Company** you represent, and **YOU**! That's *"Right"*, YOU are serving the *Customer*, the *Company*, and *Yourself*

Now, let's define the word *"Service"*; to give "service" is to *'help'*, *'assist'*, *'examine'*, or to *'repair'*. All these issues require honest and *"true compassion"* towards people, and not considering them as just *"Customers"*.

Stating that a *"Customer"* does not need to be serviced may sound like a contradiction in terms, although *"service"* is NOT what a" Customer" needs, due to the fact that what they **need** and **want** is *"Resolution"* with *"Complete Satisfaction"* to *"their benefit"* This can only be achieved when a *"Customer"* is *industriously* and *authentically* **cared for** and **about**...Hence the term *"Customer Care"*.

It is imperative to fully understand the importance of *"Customer Service"* and how it *"custom fits"* in the process of doing *"What's Right" in You.*

Once a person enters your establishment, he now becomes a... *"Customer/Guest/Prospect/Opportunity"* with *particular* needs and wants, and his expectations must be met. A **connection** must be *initiated*, again, *from the very beginning* with that "one" individual. Ensuring that "one" individual experiences a *"**Feeling of appreciation**"* of YOU serving him and a clear-cut awareness of the *"**importance**"* of his existence. By simply giving him the *"**Service**"* that he *wants, expects,* and *deserves,* makes this principle a no brainer. It all begins with a genuine smile and an *"enthusiastic attitude"* and knowing how to do your job *efficiently* and *effectively*.

The focus here is this; an interaction is taking place between two parties, and when one of those parties is dependant on the other, the best foot must be put forward with *sincere* and *empathetic "reason",* with consistent and friendly conduct. Now, it could be that the person being served is in a bad mood and really does not want to comply due to the situation at hand, or merely has extremely high expectations due to whatever it is that he has or is experiencing. Early on I stated that *it's* **ALL** about *"The Customer"* and it starts with YOU, and this is still very accurate. Although, being that it all starts with YOU...YOU must first get a strong grip-hold on relating to *"Customers"* with *positive* and *conducive-*behavior. Being fully aware that a *complete* and *comprehensive* attitude is required. *Problem Solving* to *"**The Customer's Complete Satisfaction**"*!

It does not matter what type of business that one is in, if YOU are committed to a **profession** of meeting *"face-to-face"* or have been positioned in a *"one-on-one"* scenario and YOU have accepted that position of responsibility, YOU have to actually put "yourself" in a very vulnerable position, because the person in front of YOU has the *"Initiated-control",* and it is now your responsibility to ensure that this person, or persons are **served** with the *"utmost potential"* of not only what YOU can bring to the table, but most importantly, *"The Company"* that YOU are backing-up. I am sure that any "Company' that YOU are representing has all the **"proper policies"** and *"Customer Procedures"* intact to ensure *"Complete Satisfaction"!*

Procedure 1 — Customer Relations & Relationships

"Complete Satisfaction"

It seems that many *"Company Policies"* miss the mark in their *"Policy Awareness Structure"* ...and this is due to the fact that the *"right"* hand does not always know what the left hand is doing most of the time. This of course is due to poor communication, or a lack there of. To *"communicate"* is to **connect** by being *in touch* with whom YOU are conversing with and being ready to **"serve"** the situation to Complete Satisfaction!

Here's an example of the **"What's Right"** *"Company Policy Process"* ...

With our guests we will Recognize that "Customers" are the beginning of our success with no end in sight, and that nothing good happens until we satisfy every need and concern of our guests! Ensuring that each guest's expectations are exceeded for Service, Process, Product, Quality, Price and Value! With an Outcome of "Complete Satisfaction", and a will to Recommend by incorporating a Confident Feeling of Gratification and Satisfaction while interacting with our Company to promote positive word of mouth advertising and to develop "Lifetime Relationships", where "100% Complete Satisfaction" and a "Good Time" is our determination! Always ensuring that each guest feels Authentically Appreciated and Welcomed, by handling each inquiry, concern, and complaint, with a Respectful, Courteous, Fair, and Prompt manner, always to the guest's "Complete Satisfaction"! To exude a Reputation as a "Model Company" through community and charity involvement while establishing Meaningful Relationships!

The groundwork for establishing a grand opportunity for **"Complete Satisfaction"** in a *"Customer"* in this **"Betterment Selling"** process, it not only begins with a "welcoming hello", but also incorporated into the mix, is a simple ***"Thank You"*** from the very beginning. Indicating an *"attitude of appreciation"*!

Showing and stating your **"appreciation"** ("Positive Reception") to *"The Customer"* for giving YOU the *"opportunity"* to <u>serve</u> them in your place of business from the get-go! Not waiting until <u>YOU</u> get something out of it, like a sale. As long as your **"motives"** are for ***"Right Reason"***, "YOU" will achieve an *"Instinctive Connection"*, and **"the sale will prevail"** and or, your *"Customer"* will be ***"Completely Satisfied and Will Definitely Recommend"***!

We all know how to make a connection with a *"Customer"* at one point or another, but I have to ask, have YOU ever "connected integrally" with a *"Customer"* from the very beginning of your selling process? I'm sorry to say that in most cases, NOT! The reason I so adamantly state, NOT, is due to the fact that most do not know what the term meaning is, to be **"Integral"**. If YOU fall into this category, allow me to be of assistance.

Everything that I am indicating in this **"Betterment Process"** has a tendency to go full circle, for this *"Reason"*! You're going to get a kick out of this, if nothing else for its <u>simplicity</u>; The term ***"Integral is a*** *"Fundamental Connection"*, *'internally'* in the *'central'* part of one's self, opening the door to a *'basic'* and *'vital'* <u>function</u>, and understanding it is... *"at the* **"Heart"** *of"*, that truly matters! Here's the simplicity... The key missing ingredient in so many cases... is **"Heart"**!

Not only meeting *'face-to-face'* or *'one-on-one'* does **"Customer Relationships"** begin, but it is also being earnestly ***'mindful'***, seeing ***'eye-to-eye'***, and ***'heart-to-heart'***!

I term this as...

Procedure 1 — Customer Relations & Relationships

"Integral Connections"!!!

NOTE: It is the *"Complete Responsibility"* of *"The Company"* that employs the situation where *"Customers"* are the *"Chief Ingredient"* to their success. To <u>comprehend</u> and <u>implement</u> this **ACTION** to get it *"Right"!*

"RIGHT REASON!"

Not meaning to be redundant, but for the sake of stating its importance to

"The Betterment Process"!

Right: *(adv.) accurate (adj.) respectable (adj.) moral (adj.) genuine (v.) restore (n) entitlement*

Reason: *(n.) motive (v.) goal (n.) intelligence (v.) rationalizes (n.) senses (v.) persuade*

It is very imperative that this part of the equation is fully understood and *Appreciated*, as well as *"Accepted"* and put into *"Action"*!

There's those straight **A's** again.

Here is a simple equation for YOU... It's in an algebraic form, although has absolutely nothing to do with algebra...

$K + A = P$, and $K - A = O$...

*"**K**nowledge plus **A**ction equals **P**rofit, yet YOU can have all the **K**nowledge in the World, if YOU minus **A**ction, YOU get absolutely **Z**ero!*

Think about it and pass it on!

Knowing and even understanding the *"**Integral Principles**"* of this *"**Betterment Process**"*, it is of absolutely no use, if it is not integrated into your *"**Plan of Action**"*, and put into *"**Action**"* with sincere *"**Heart'***...Once done so, 'Purpose' and or...

*"**Objectives will be Achieved Inevitably**"!*

Now I understand that the success of any business requires tight margins in many categories that must always be met and out of the red, also known as *"the bottom line"*. It is also understood that *"**The Bottom Line**"* is the most important element to any Company's success and *"Prosperous Growth"*. But if any person in an upper decision-making position will earnestly grasp and incorporate *"Heart Making Decisions"*, these *"Principle Choices"* will only enhance the growth of any *"Customer Retention & Referral Program"*! Where in turn, the 'Objectives' that are attached to one's responsibilities will leave that "One" (YOU)... Completely Satisfied!!!

Allow me to introduce to YOU a poem of which I have penned as...

*"**Integral Connections**", face-to-face, one-on-one.*

Now here's a mini-test to check your '*open-mind*' and thinking *outside the box.* Which will require a keen '*perception*', and not a '*deception*' Other than the words in the poem and the way the words are laid out, what do YOU see?

Do YOU see a wine goblet, or 2 profile faces facing each other?

Here's a hint for YOU...the topic of this process does not involve wine, nor the consumption thereof. Although a glass of Chablis doesn't sound bad.

Integral Connections

"Face to Face" & "One on One"

"Integral Connections"

"Mind to Mind"
Is to Be Aware of
a Connection of Reason
a Common Ground We'll Find
When "WE SEE" Things

"Eye to Eye"
To Join in a Similar Fashion
To Be on the Same Level of
Vision & Passion
Creating a Bond
not to Fear It…

But from
"Heart to Heart"
It's a Joining of Spirit,
Strengths and Compassion,
Not Only
"Face to Face"
But
Champion to Champion

By Patrick St. John

What's Right
*Doing it For "The Customer"
Not to, "The Customer"*

Procedure 2
The Customer
"Who is Truly # 1"

In the *Prologue* of this Procedure, a pertinent question has been brought up about...

"Who Truly is #1?"

Unfortunately, most people may ask, if they are inquisitive enough to want to know about a *"Customer"*, they may begin with; *"What, is a Customer"?* When *"empathetic reason"* is utilized, the question is actually; *"Who, is a Customer"?*

Two topics arise here that are of utmost importance and must be accepted with full comprehension and then incorporated into *"Action Awareness"*!

Empathy and *Reason*...

"Reason" is defined as *'motive', 'intelligence', 'sanity', 'persuasion', 'deduction'* or *"underlying principle"*, and the underlying *"principle"* is a law of true *"moral ethics"*, which only makes sense when dealing with people (*"Customers"*). No matter how much the word *'reason'* is researched, there is nothing to be found that indicates excuses. I'm just saying!

"Empathy" is defined as *understanding* or, believe it or not, *compassion*...that's right compassion. When combining these two very imperative *prerequisites*, one begins to identify with and have the *compassion/empathy* that is the central ingredient to understanding what a *"Customer"* is all about and the importance of *consideration* and *appreciation* for *"The Customer"*, for without any one "Customer", you have **"NOTHING"**!

When dealing with people one truly has to go beyond the term *"Customer"* and accept the fact that they are *"People"*, people with *feelings, wants, desires, and needs*. It is an honest *"Customer Relationship"* attitude (compassion) that must be one's main *objective* toward a <u>*"Customer's Complete Satisfaction"*</u>, as well as <u>your own</u>!

Which is the beginning process of "Inevitable Success", or...

"Achieving Your Objectives Inventively"!

Now let's dig a little deeper on the subject ***"The Customer"*** by asking ourselves...

"Who is a "Customer"?

A *"Customer"* is <u>*you*</u> or <u>*me*</u>, a <u>*friend*</u>, a <u>*neighbor*</u>, a <u>*relative*</u>, a <u>*co-worker*</u>, a <u>*church member*</u>, a <u>*club member*</u>, etc. One thing for certain is that all of these examples have one very important thing in common, and that is that they all are *relational*, or have some *"in common factors"* when it *relates* to <u>*relationships*</u>. A connection must be achieved, and reputable in order for a "relationship" to be established and moved in a positive direction and or existence! The best way to grasp this would be to put yourself in the position of how You would like to be treated as a guest in someone's home. I would assume that everyone would like to be treated with *respect* and *appreciation*, as one would be treated as a "GUEST" in our own home. Two more very *imperative* subjects have now arisen, and those are **connections** and **relationships**. When an equation is used that involves the <u>understanding</u> and the <u>importance</u> of *"relationships"*, this is the beginning of a straightforward **"connection"** toward the *"Relationship Building Process"* with a *"Customer"*.

All *"Customers"* have the <u>Right</u> to be who they are at any given time and where they want to be at any given time...as the old adage goes, *"the customer is always right!"*, and that's OK, because they have the money and the <u>connections</u>

(connection to their own selves to make decisions)! So be aware of their *"rights"*, by simply listening to what they are actually saying, and not what you may want to hear or wish they were saying. By simply using this *"strategy/process/awareness"*, you won't have to deal with any **wrongs**, but only" *"Rights"*!

Now, what are *"Rights"* and what are *"Wrongs"* when it pertains to a *"Customer"*?

"Rights" are construed as having *'privileges'* or certain *'liberties*. These privileges include being treated with *'earnest'* **respect** (value), and just as important, *'appreciation'* or *"**positive reception**"* (discussed in more detail in Procedure 3). By understanding and fully accepting the fact that *"**Value**"* is just as important as *"The Customer"*! Now what you have is a *"Valued Customer"*, combined, they are one in the same which equates to *"***worth***"*. So now ask yourself...*What is a customer's worth*? Take a moment, and pause... take a deep breath, and think about it; We'll get back to this topic in just a moment.... Now let's cover the topic of *"wrongs"* ...

"Wrongs" are defined as being *'incorrect'*, *'unethical'*, *'unjust'*, *'damaging'*, *'amiss'*, and even *'dishonorable'*. I don't think anyone in a career that involves *"face to face"* or *"One on One"* communications, wants to do anything incorrect or dishonorable in their profession... Especially when their livelihood depends on it. Now I mention *"one's livelihood"*.

Did you take a brief moment to think about the above question? *"What is a customer's worth"*? ...Is it a one-time shot? An opportunity to make a quick buck and move on to the next victim, or is it the beginning of a long-lasting (never-ending bond), *"relationship"*? In order to achieve a strong bond with any one person, "it takes two to tango", and most would think that the *process* begins with "YOU", when actually *"the process"* begins with *"The Customer"*, although it is You that must first initiate and accept that with-out anyone "*Customer*", you have nothing, and "*the customer is always right*"!

Now, you may find a contradictory statement here, indicating that "*the process begins with the customer*", when one is normally led to believe it begins with YOU, well just keep your focus on "*The Customer*", and everything else (Numbers, Surveys, Return and Referred Business, etc.) will be "*achieved inevitably*"! How? You may ask. With a "*positive attitude*", and this "Betterment Process", being that "*attitude*" means everything, and I think we all know that. "I hope, continue reading.

"**The Customer's** *tangible* **worth/value**" is never-ending, which makes them a "*Tangible Asset*", take gold for example. Ask yourself, "Would I treat a hundred-plus pounds of gold with disrespect or lack of regard for its **worth**?" I think you get my point. When "*The Customer*" is always put first and is considered **#1** from the get-go, YOU can't lose...

Let's cover things that have "*great value*" ...

- Family
- Your Significant Other
- Your Home
- Your Job/Career
- Gold
- Money
- Beliefs
- YOU

...Now ask yourself another question; "Would I take advantage and not *appreciate* the *significance* that any one of these "*valuable assets*" had to offer, and then not give them my fullest and utmost **honest attention**?" If your "*main objective*" was to nurture (*nurture* is to '*cherish*' and '*care-for*'), and enjoy the benefits that they had to offer YOU and everyone involved, and providing that YOU are true to YOU, the answer is an emphatic, "**NO**"!

Here is another minor quiz...Did you notice under the category list of *"great value"* that *"The Customer"* was not listed? If you did catch this omission, then you are understanding the *"true process"* of getting the task at hand completed. Oops, I did it again, did you catch it? When it comes to *"The Customer"*, there is never a completed course, but only a beginning and a forward momentum with *compassion* and *integrity*! And where YOU guide, they will follow! The reason *"The Customer"* was omitted from the list above, is due to the way things are currently being done in most businesses. *"The Customer"* is not truly considered a *"Valued Asset"*, for the long run that is, but unfortunately for a one-time shot for a huge *profit*. Sure, some companies will implement incentive programs to generate extra business, such as *"referral fees"* (birddogs), *"survey bonuses"* and such, but they always seem temporary or not highly encouraged on a consistent basis.

Notice out of the 8 *'great values'*, 6 are in a category of growth when it pertains to the connectivity of other people...

- Family
- Your Significant Other
- Your Home
- Your Job/ Career
- Beliefs
- You

Let's go back to the beginning for a moment. "Who is a Customer"? Let's connect the dots... A "Customer" is you, me , a friend , a neighbor , a relative , a co-worker , a church member , a club member , etc...

- **Family:** *Relatives/Everyone they know*
- **Your Significant Other:** *Family/Friends/Co-workers*
- **Your Home:** *Neighbors/Everyone they know.*
- **Your Job/Career:** *Co-workers/Everyone they know.*
- **Beliefs:** *Church Members, Bible Studies, Meetings, etc.*
- **YOU:**

I think you get my point. We all have that one in common factor. Oh…I forgot YOU… **YOU:** *Friends*, *Family*, *Neighbors*, *everyone you meet*. Notice that all the above examples (assets) mentioned have connections with other people (*Opportunities*) that have **connections** with other people (*Potential Customers*).

Here is another imperative facet of the process of *"What's Right"*, and I call it the *"R. & R. effect"* (Retain and Refer) or "R & R-ing the Customer". As long as you always remember to put *"The Customer"* first, and focus on their needs and wants, *"Complete Satisfaction"* will be achieved and now you can do your own *"R & R-ing"* (*Rest and Relaxation*), because you are beginning to *'achieve your objectives inevitably*! But don't stop now your on a roll…*"Winning"*!!!

It's a continuous cycle that truly never ends, unless YOU allow it, and that my friend will lead to a dreadful conclusion, if you don't get it" Right*"*! That is why it is so imperative not only to understand the process of knowing *"What's Right"*, but more importantly, putting it into <u>action</u>. <u>**Always**</u> position *"The Customer"* <u>first</u>!

I promise you…it will be a *"Win, Win, Win"*, for *"The Customer"*," *YOU"*, and *"The Company"* that YOU <u>represent</u>!

Now that we have covered "*who a customer is*", let's determine <u>what</u> a *Customer is*", or is it <u>what</u> a "*Customer/Consumer*" **<u>wants</u>**. Being a customer is no different than you or I. You, and I, <u>are</u> a "*Customer/Consumer*" at one time or another, and don't we all <u>want</u> the same thing as a "*Customer/Consumer*" that is in front of You?

Listed below are 10 typical "*wants*" of a *Customer/Consumer*...

- Respect
- Courtesy
- Appreciation
- Consideration
- Trust
- Complete Satisfaction
- Attention
- Value
- Benefit
- They "*want*" what <u>they</u> "*want*", when <u>they</u> "*want* it*"

I listed these typical *wants* in the order that works best for me when dealing with "*Customers/Consumers*", although being that we are all different in our own unique way, take a moment and list them in the order that you feel has worked or would work best for You, providing that You do not step out of the "*proper process*" box, (*this is <u>all about</u> and <u>for</u> "The Customer"*)!

Note: Notice the words underlined in the caption above...Think about it.

When this type of awareness exists and is utilized on a consistent basis, **relationships** begin to form, and *success* prevails for all involved!

As this *"procedure"* concludes...all sounds great for *"The Customer"*, but one might ask..." What about me"?

A couple of *"position statements"* indicated throughout this writing are, **"*Inevitable Success*"** or" ***Accomplishing Your Objectives Inevitably"***!

"Objectives"

"Objectives" come in many shapes and sizes, or levels of importance, and based on your level of *'priority consciousness'*, YOU may have to take baby steps and work on the simpler things that are easier to *manage* and *focus* on. This is where your *'Positive Energy'* level and enhanced aura can excel. Most people focus on the large or overwhelming *objectives* and get all stressed out, which lowers your *"positive aura state of sub-consciousness"*. This usually demonstrates a desperate or muddled demeanor that is somewhat exasperated due to the level of thought and *responsibility* of *"Obligatory.*

Commitments", which also creates a blurred focus on what or who really matters. So, what one needs to do is *prioritize, rationalize,* and *determine* the level of *importance* that your *obligations* may fall under. Your first obligation is YOU, just as only one *"Customer"* makes all the difference in the world, so do YOU!

Get this... more times than not, when one obligation is achieved usually another one will be achieved, therefore other obligations are negated by simply achieving the latter. Here's the point...

Focus on YOU first, because after all, YOU should be your first *obligation/commitment* to a ***"Betterment Process"*** to earning a *Prospect/Customer's* worth (business), and turning them into an **"Owner"**, *proud* and *enthusiastic* to not only spend their hard-earned money with YOU but also willing to spread *__the word__*! When this is succeeded for the *"Right Reason"*, then "Number Objectives", 100% Completely Satisfied Surveys and 5 Star Reviews will be ...

"Accomplished Automatically/Inevitably"!

Numbers are very crucial to all involved...but for *"The Customer"*, it's <u>value</u> and succeeding in achieving *"Complete Satisfaction"* in their venture! For the *"Representative"*, and or *"The Company"* being represented, it involves several other aspects...

- Volume Sales
- Gross Profit
- Net Profit
- Surveys/Reviews
- Incentives
- Contests
- Quotas
- Margins
- Customer Retention
- Employee Retention
- Buying Power

All the above *objectives* are *attainable* when the *'proper focus'* and **motives** are put into **action** for the ***"Right Reason"***, and you'll feel better for doing ***"What's Right"*** in ***You***, for *"The Customer"*. Trust me they'll sincerely appreciate it, and with your ***__continued assistance__*** and '*communication*' with them, they will also enroll themselves into the *"Customer Referral Program"!* Especially when they have an experience that indicates that it is them, that this process is all about. Hence the term…

"Doing it For The Opportunity and Not to, The Opportunity"!

Here is a prime example of the importance of a Customer's Complete Satisfaction relating to the "Car Business" (Auto Sales). Being that a car purchase is the second highest expense that a Consumer spends their dollars on. A house being the highest purchase. Surveys rank #1 when it comes to an assurance that these auto Consumers are satisfied with their experience. This "*survey structure*" is so pertinent to their success that it holds a top of the list priority to all involved! It is known as a "***Customer Satisfaction Index***" (CSI). This protocol is of the utmost importance due to the fact that the Automobile makers need and want "***Customer Retention***". Being that there are 157 Automobile Manufacturing Businesses in the US as of 2023 with 0% decline from 2022. It's a no wonder why this process is so essential "*Earned Customers*" are chosen at random and then surveyed. This survey index entails several categories, i.e.

- *Salesperson,*
- *Finance Person,*
- *Delivery process,*
- *Vehicle*

This is only a portion of this required course of action. It also includes a Yes and No portion of satisfaction, i.e.

- *Problem Free Delivery*
- *Vehicle Problems*
- *Full Tank of Gas*
- *Follow-Up Contact*

- *Satisfied with Contact*
- *Return to Dealership*
- *Recommend Dealership*
- *Comment Section*

It is the hope to all involved that this "Survey' comes in at a...

100% Complete Satisfaction and Will Definitely Recommend!

Now, let me break in down why it is so important to achieve a 100% survey to All involved. First the Salesperson; At most dealerships there are cash incentives/bonus involved providing that a salesperson achieves a National or Regional average. This percentage average is usually 94% to 98%, which can be considered relatively high, being that no one is perfect. Therefore a 100% Regional average is a target virtually impossible to hit. As long as the Salesperson achieves Regional averages in an annual quarter, he or she will obtain substantial "Annual Bonuses", and at the same time The Dealership gains their targeted clout, giving them "Buying Power". Which entails a greater inventory selection upon ordering, as well as earned Dealership Cash Incentives that can be an incentive given to the Customer/Consumer. Termed, "Dealer Cash". This "Dealer-*Cash*" can also open a window of $$$ to the Salesperson, over and beyond annual "***Manufacturer Bonuses***"! Now giving YOU more Buying Power!

With this detailed information of a "*Customer Survey*" and its high level of importance and even consequences, it leads us to...

"The Customer's Perspective"

It would only be fair to look at things from *"The Customer's"* point of view, and at the same time give you a better picture of what may be happening on the other side of the fence, so to speak.

When a person (*Consumer/Prospect*) sets out on a *"Purchasing Journey"*; notice that I did not say…" Go Shopping". Why? you might ask. People do not get up out of their *"Comfort Zone"* just to spin their wheels and jump through hoops, unless they have an *"earnest desire"* to possess a product or service. They may give the impression that they are merely shopping around or may have just started their *"shopping process"*, (*"Purchasing Process"*). This is where your trained and skilled awareness kicks in. You need to fully understand that there is no such thing as a *"Shopper"*, only a *"Buyer"* collecting information to make the *"best decision"* possible that fulfills all *"their benefits"*, and or needs to make that *"final decision"* to **"*OWN*"**. That's *"right"* **Own,** not "BUY" …Nobody wants to buy anything, but merely *"OWN"* something or everything to their **Complete Satisfaction**!

What is *"Complete Satisfaction"*? It is the *"pleasure of fulfilling an agreement" with "complete happiness"*!

Let's take a moment and expand on the two words of which are underlined in the last statement, first; **satisfaction;** (*n.*) *'approval', 'pleasure', 'fulfillment', 'contentment',* **'agreement'**, etc.

Now, let's dig even deeper and expand on one being **satisfied**, with another noun putting a different perspective on the importance of "**satisfaction**"; (*n.*) *'redress'*, (pronounced re-dress) The word "**redress**" is not a commonly used word, although it is a requirement for a complete perception of satisfaction and accentuates that **satisfaction to completeness**!

As defined in Merriam Webster's Dictionary; to *'redress'*, *"is to make right"*!

Here are some similar words to making things right; (*v.*) *'restore'*, *'equalize'*, *'rectify'*, *'remedy'*, *'right'*, *'put right'*, *'even out'*, *'balance out'*, etc.

It is my hope that with this directive, You will have a stronger comprehension of what it is to have **"SATISFACTION!"**

You may have noticed that the last word that has in common factors with **satisfaction,** is **'*Agreement*';** (*n'*) *'conformity'*, *'harmony'*, *'union'*, *'covenant'*, *'promise'*,*' pact'*, *'understanding'*, *'settlement'*, *'bargain'*, etc.

"To be in agreement" or *"come into agreement"*, common ground must be established with *integrity, transparency, focus, time, commitment, compassion, harmony, concurrence, unity, conformity, and even negotiation.* Your reputation will depend on it! Without an agreement, whether it be at the beginning of the process or at the *"resolution"* part of the process of solving one's problem/objective or earning one's business (Close of the sale)! *"Resolution Process"* to be discussed in more detail in Process #7, *"Making it Happen"*!

"Reputation"

"Customers" rely on one thing: *"Trust"*. *"Customers"* are no different than you or I. We all want to be treated with *respect,* which builds **"trust"**! People spend their money (*Buy/Own*) with whom they like, and we all know we can only like someone we *"trust"*.

Don't fall victim to the trap or *"reputation"* of being looked at as a *shyster, villain, vulture* or, well, compared to an attorney, if you will…All the "lawyer" jokes, I think you get my drift! My apologies if by chance you are associated in any way to an attorney personally or are one. Although attorneys are very astute in knowing what is really going on, and how to handle the situation at hand with a successful defense and presentation with the hope of a successful outcome for their client. Did YOU get that, *"for their client"!* If one is not doing it for the *Client/Customer* they are putting themselves and the Company of which they are representing in a very vulnerable position to fall under their own feet and land in pile of *"Bad Rap Reputation"*! If this takes place it is not only a disservice to any profession but also makes it much more difficult to obtain and maintain objectives.

Here's another *'thought pattern'* example that people (*Consumers*) fall into about *"Sales People"* ..." Politicians", who say what one wants to hear, and gives *false promises*. It is because of this that people (*Consumers*) get into these *'paradigms'*, or ideas of stereotyping certain professions and or persons. Unfortunately, sales *professionals* and front counter *associates* take the *"bad rap"* from the get-go. Starting with an up-hill battle, and in some cases, are never even given a opportunity to position themselves to voice their innocence and possibly good intentions!

Never *assert* yourself in a way that may imply that YOU are in any way associated with attorney or politician's *tactics* that are a *paradigm* in a Customer's mind, but YOU need not be intimidated in any way either…Don't be shy, be *humble,* and yet *proud* to inform who YOU actually are, and the Company YOU represent, also indicating that YOU are on **their side**! In other words, create and establish a *"Paradigm Shift"* in the way a *Customer* is reacting and or responding. Change the way they are thinking and redirect them so that there is a complete understanding that it is THEY that truly matters, and it is YOU that will be the **One** who will satisfy all their concerns and objectives to *"Complete Satisfaction"*!

Be *'authentic'* and *'reputable'* from the very first Hello. It's that *"First Impression"* that "breaks the ice". Now here's another contradictory term for YOU; *"break the ice"*. I have seen it where company professionals actually create thin ice with a *Customer* as they are "breaking the ice". Now the *"Company's Protocol"* (REPUTATION) is thrown out the window from the very beginning, due to the fact that now, *"The Customer"* and, *"The Company Representative"* are proceeding on thin ice, and if any *Company* allows this type of beginning, the *Company's Protocol* is now in question. When any *"Professional"* guides their *"Guest"* along a path on thin ice, that thin ice will surely break and give way to a very *devastating* and *disappointing* **END**! So, the moral is this...Just be **"Reputable"** and use ice in your beverages!

Always remember that it is **YOU** that holds the reins, not only on YOU, but just as **'*relevant*'**, it is YOU that also holds the reins to the...

"Company's Reputation"!

It is a reputation that can make or break one's success. Once a reputation is established, good, bad, or indifferent, it is hard to change, especially in this day and age with social networking and social media, where reviews are right at your fingertips, literally! It used to be word of mouth, whereas now it is a word in print reaching who knows how many people at one time, and if it's a bad "rep", people will have a tendency to push the envelope even harder and further reaching even more people that may be inquisitive to know about a company or transaction that may have recently taken place! So always be conscience of what type of reputation you want to establish in yourself and the company that you represent. By establishing a positive and successful reputation for yourself and the company of which you are representing will catapult you to the **"*Retain* and *Refer*"** process! Where once You hit the referral hot button in the *"Customer Relationship"* that

You established and maintained, your position now becomes much easier to navigate to the "*road of success*"!

Here are some National statistics that have been in place for decades in the face-to face sales process…On average a fresh walk-in to this type of sales process will be sold or closed at an average of a 25% ratio, as where a referred customer will be sold at an average of a 75% closing-ratio. At this significant ratio differential, it is obvious that one will work significantly harder in the attempt to earn one's business in a non-referral process. So, what the relevance being made here is very obvious that a **Retain and Refer** (R&R) process is an imperative element in the "*Betterment Process*" of doing "*What's Right*!" More on this subject matter in Procedure #8 (Branding the Brain and the 7 R's)

What's Right
Doing it For "The Opportunity"
Not to, "The Opportunity"

Procedure 3
Greet & Meet
"The Customer"
"Relationship Creation"

Notice that this part of the *"What's Right"* process is different than what is most common. Normally this process is called *"meet & greet"*. One does not meet then greet somebody. You don't even have to think about it...You know it...You *"Greet"*, then you *"Meet"*. Once You meet, it seems to start with a *"handshake"*.

Here's some interesting data for YOU. It was determined in a study compiled by the University of Manchester that 70% of people don't even know what a *"handshake"* is truly all about, why we do it, or even where it derived from...

...It has become so *ubiquitous*, and somewhat surprising that such a high percentage of people, statistically speaking, are not informed or educated on *"The Handshake"*, being that we all do it. One might even ask, "what has actually become of the *"Handshake?"* Has it really come to where, it's merely, *"monkey-see, monkey do"*, without any meaning or *conviction?"*

There are many different *"greeting/welcoming"* customs around the world that have absolutely nothing to do with a *"handshake"*. In New Zealand, people greet each other by touching noses; In Ethiopia, men touch shoulders; In many Asian countries, people bow to each other; The Democratic Republic, male friends touch foreheads upon greeting; Arab and many European countries, welcoming and greeting customs entail hugs and kisses on the cheek.

While this was not always the norm, the most prevalent and common form of greeting one another around the world is now *"The Handshake"*.

"The Origin of the Handshake"

For information purposes, and being that I have now baited your curiosity, I find it only fair that YOU are enlightened of how *"The Handshake"* originated and developed.

There are several theories of where, how, and why *"The Handshake"* derived…Through thorough research, the one that makes the most *"sense"* to me is dates back to prehistoric times, when hunters would come across one another, they would extend their arm forward and show that their hand/hands held no weapon, and then the two would meet hands in a friendly gesture. Staying on the same note, the most popular theory indicates a gesture of peace between soldiers dating back to the 5th Century in Ancient Greece during the Roman era, also showing that no weapon was present, and when the 2 met hands, which was actually a gripping each one's forearm, and then shaking up and down to ensure that no weapon/weapons were concealed. As time passed and societies changed, concealed weapons and such no longer became a concern or threat. *"The Handshake"* has been maintained as a greeting gesture as well as a man's word, or promise! Now what does that mean in today's society?

What's in a Handshake?

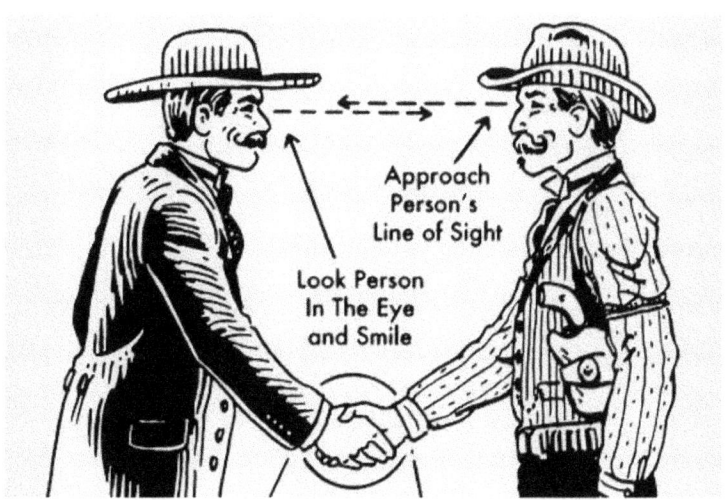

Seems simple enough; *"What actually is in a Handshake?"*, why and how do we do it?... We have actually never really been educated that a *"Handshake"* is so much more than merely a practice, or just grabbing the other person's hand and shaking the hell out of it. Although we have been taught that that is the first thing we do when we *meet & greet,* or *"greet & meet"* someone, and this is why we think, we normally do...

"The Handshake"!

First, let's take note or an extra effort, and focus on all of the *'pertinent surroundings'* that may pertain to the situation calling for a *"handshake;* who are you shaking hands with...a man or a woman. Are they a small or a big person...Do they seem jovial, skeptical, or down in the dumps...It is *imperative* that YOU are aware of these *characteristics* before you enter *"their space"* and shake their hand, as well as having your motives in-check!

Some people may not want to shake your hand, or at least give the impression that this is the case.

I will never forget my first genuine lesson in the importance and relevance of a *"Handshake"* ...

"It was at the very beginning of my *"Customer Relations"* career when I was very apprehensive to just walk up to a stranger *"face to face"* and enter **"their space"** ... (which I will discuss in further detail later in this process message/lesson)

...Here I was working for a company that peddled the 3rd. highest price ticket item that most people spend their hard-earned dollars on (furniture), and fresh out of high school with only 6 months of Business College under my belt and totally wet behind the ears (a green pea) when it came to greeting and _meeting_ someone in a *"face-to-face"*, *"one-on-one" contact/communication* scenario. Being that my only experience relating to a *"Consumer"* face-to-face was as a shoe salesman at a "Thom McCann" shoe store during the summer of my sophomore year of High School, and when it comes to selling shoes, not too many hands are involved.

Anyway, I was instructed to shake everyone's hand that I welcome to our establishment with _face-to-face_ contact/ communication. I simply asked my mentor; "What if they don't want to shake my hand?" and he replie*d, "That's easy, as you are verbalizing your greeting, put out your hand and if the Guest/Consumer does not respond with the normal response by reaching out and meeting your hand, then you have to initiate..."* I was to actually reach out and grab the *Guest/Prospect/Opportunity's* hand and *"take control"* of the situation while maintaining a *positive* and non-intimidating *demeanor*.

Well this particular day and scenario finally arrived, and as I approached this *Guest/Prospect/Opportunity* at the front door with a very apprehensive demeanor due to the fact that I was very young and naïve and put in the position to not only relate to *"People/Consumers"*, but actually make a '*connection*' so that they would want to spend their time and hard earned dollars with me, and to my surprise this *Prospect* was just as befuddled as I was in that moment. Although by me *"**taking control**"* of the situation, the *Guest/Prospect/Opportunity* was so overwhelmed by my *enthusiasm* and authentic *excitement* that he came into our store, he found it easy to comply with everything that

I asked him and directed him toward.

He understood that he was *important* to me, and *"The Company"*, and that my true interest was in his interests, and even concerns to his *"Complete Satisfaction"!* The other lesson that I learned here was the importance of *physical contact*, this goes one step further than just the *aura* that is taking place, but actually strengthens that *aura*. Which enhances the *"relationship building"* process with *honesty* and *trust*.

Think about it when some stranger walks up and **"meets & greets"** you at a place of your choosing and finds that may have a *reputation* of not truly being on your side, or maybe that stranger gives that impression themselves. Would YOU trust that <u>stranger</u> to <u>care</u> for your **"wants & needs"**? Yes, that person is a stranger. Now switch shoes, you are now that stranger, but not an <u>unrelated</u> stranger. How are you <u>related</u>? You are the person that *represents* the **"Company"** and or **"Product"** that they are **interested** in or **compelled** by, and from the very beginning of a <u>"Buyer's"</u> **"Purchasing Quest"**, they already have a small amount of trust instilled in them. Because they would not be where they did not want to be, nor would they be standing in front of YOU, a stranger. But always remember that they are there <u>**"for them"**</u>, and not YOU!

Set it in concrete that **"The Handshake"** has so much more to offer than merely a gesture, or motion that we go through. So please don't exploit *"The Handshake"*, which is most commonly recognized as a *ritual* or a *practice* so much so, that it becomes merely a habit... How insensitive is that!

It's a very sad day when one is not taking advantage of what we have been given so gracefully and naturally...The ability to <u>**"connect"**</u> (*Aura Creation or Impression Connection*), and the capability to acquire and create experiences (*memories*). I don't think that it's because anyone has disrespect for the, or a *"handshake'*, one may simply not be aware if it's connotation and importance at the beginning of a... <u>**"Customer Relationship Building Process.**</u>

When one is not properly informed what a *"handshake"* is truly all about, it becomes a hindrance to One's gift of *"awareness abilities"* (*the 5 senses*), and the gift to communicate them properly and for the *"Right Reason"*. This my comrade in arms is an innocent tragedy. So, I am going to entitle this as a; *"Hand-shake Strategy"* instead of a *"Hand-shake Tragedy"* ...

"The Positive Reception Handshake"!

In the Procedure 2, I mentioned *"positive reception"*, this is actually where the term "UP" derived from; It is not merely getting up-off your keester, but it's being *'up-beat'*, *'ready'*, and *'optimistic'* in your welcoming approach. Take pleasure in your greeting with *enthusiasm, vigor,* and most importantly, *"perceptive awareness"*! Due to the fact that it all starts at the beginning with a **"simple smile"**, a *"sincere handshake"*, a sincere **Thank You,** nice to meet you and **"welcome"**; NOT a, "can I hep ya"?

Here's an example of a *"Positive Reception"* ...

From a short distance You have already *"greeted"* Your *Guest/Consumer* (opportunity/future Customer) with a *friendly, jovial, confident,* and **welcoming** demeanor by simply saying **hello** and **welcome** to ABC Motors" (*as you get closer in your approach, use good timing to arrive in their presence or space so that you smoothly segue into a* **"Formal Meeting"** *with a* **"Handshake"**). For example...

Rep; *"Hello, welcome to ABC Motors, how's it going today? (from a distance as you approach)*

Guest: *"Pretty good, thanks!*

Rep: *"Well **thank you** for stopping in, my name is Patrick, and you are?"* (Handshake)

Guest: *"John"*

Procedure 3 — Greet & Meet

Rep: *"Nice to **'meet'** you John, so how may I be of assistance **for you** today?"*

Guest: *"I'm just looking!"*

Rep: *"Well that's awesome John, we sure appreciate you taking the time to check us out to see what we have to offer! Was there anything in particular that you're interested in looking at, or direction that I can point you in?* Note: If the prospect/consumer is somewhat reluctant or uncooperative, or just a demeanor of not wanting to be bothered, throw this in as well...*or point me in?*

Hopefully, you'll get a chuckle or a shit-eatin' grin that just might break the ice! Another brief note...laughter is always a great remedy under any derogatory situation, or at least a softener that lightens the load and changes the existent thought process that the *prospect/consumer* may be displaying in their actions and or attitude!

Once You have achieved success at this part of the *"Welcoming Reception"*, the **"Company's Guest"** and soon to be **"Customer"**, will inform you of what it is that they are interested in, and it is at this point of the **"Greet & Meet"** process you will be of great *'assistance'* and **"LEAD"** this **"Grand Opportunity"** toward **"Ownership"**, and it all begins with a **"Positive Reception"**, and an *authentic* **"Handshake"**!

Now let's discuss in more detail, **"The Handshake"** when added to a **"Positive Reception"**. The **"Positive Reception Handshake"** takes the **"handshake"** to an entirely different level of *consciousness* and **meaning**. It's actually just as important as *"The Customer"* themselves; Go figure. The *"positive reception handshake"* is not accomplished merely by your *attitude*, it is much more *profound* than that...it's **positive energy**, involving... *warmth, compassion, authenticity,* and *desire*. Focus on all of these **qualities**, then put them into **_action_** in your **_handshake_**. All these _qualities/characteristics_ are required to earnestly _connect_ and build a **_long-lasting relationship_** opportunity, under any circumstances!

Let your _Guest/Consumer_ feel the '_emotion of appreciation_' in your _"handshake"_! It all starts from hello…Having the _Guest/Consumer"_ saying… _"You Had Me From Hello"_!

After **_earning_** their business, You will then have a **_"Customer"_** saying…

I'm **_"100% Completely Satisfied and Will Definitely Recommend"_**!

(R & R…**_" Retain and Refer"!_**)

It is to Your advantage to keep Your _awareness_ in check with the **_understanding_** that in Your **_"profession"_** of **_"Customer Relations"_**, this is always Your **_"Main Objective"_**!

"Awareness"

"Awareness" is the most _"imperative component"_ in the _"Greet & Meet"_ process. When greeting and meeting a _Guest/Consumer_, the process begins way before one is even given a chance to begin a normal (stereotypical) type greeting… _"A Handshake."_

When you get out of bed in the morning you have a (full) _awareness_ that a _"committed obligation"_ is at hand, and that of course, is your job…now you may have noticed that in parentheses is the word _"full"_… _'completely'_, _'abundant'_ and _'entirely'_, have _"related relevance"_ to emphasize the fact that _"true commitment"_ is required to have the proper **_focus_** (_"to have heart"_), but first you must be '_aware_' of this _insight_ and achieve an _earnest desire_ to do **"What's Right"**, and that is to accept the fact that…

"The Customer" is <u>always first</u>!

Let's take a moment and elaborate on the term **<u>awareness</u>**…to be aware is to '_<u>acknowledge</u>_' , '_allow_', or even '_rely_' on things <u>that matter most</u> to us, and store them in a category of **<u>importance</u>** (value), when this takes place one is able to recall these things of **<u>value</u>** and act on them more _effectively_…That is if you **<u>want</u>** or **<u>desire</u>** to do **"What's Right"**…Please don't forget that it is <u>ALL</u> about **"The Customer"**, and that YOU also will come out a **"Winner"**, if you choose to follow the **"What's Right"** process!

One thing that most people are "_aware_" of, is that they **<u>desire success</u>** or want to be **<u>successful</u>**, usually at what they do for a living, or a relationship that they may be in.

Being that you are _open minded_ enough to be reading and hopefully following this **"Betterment Process"**, shows me that you fall into the category of **"successful desire"**! You must understand or be _aware_ of the fact that <u>YOU</u> are in control of your **<u>awareness</u>** and **<u>acceptance</u>** of how things get done, and are **<u>solely responsible</u>** for the outcome, because it is you that began the "_Greet & Meet_" process.

At the beginning of the "_Greet & Meet_" process it is very essential to… **"_leave your crap at the curb!_"** Most people are <u>not aware</u> that they are carrying their burdens on their shoulders, so it becomes very evident in the _aura_ that is being emitted, and then contaminates the atmosphere and diminishes, if not eliminates the "_path to success_"! If your initial "_Greet & Meet_" is unauthentic because of "_Wrong Reason_, it will be very evident in your _presentation_, not only who you are presenting yourself to be, but also in your presentation of the product that YOU represent. This does a disservice to that product and or service of which YOU are representing, and that, my friend, is also an injustice to yourself and the company that invests in you. Are you simply not aware of YOU, or are your ulterior motives askew? Think about it!

Now that your <u>awareness</u> and <u>motives</u> are in check, and I hope in <u>acceptance</u> of the <u>fact</u> that this process makes **sense**, because if not, this writing compilation will be of no use to you, and that, my friend, would be a detriment of time, and a total disservice to YOU, but if it makes *"sense"*, the time would then be well ***invested*** and ***success*** will then **triumph**! Providing this compilation is not taken in vain.

Once the decision is made to take on the **responsibility** of *"**truly caring**"* for the next *Guest/Consumer* through the door, *awareness* kicks in and tells you that you are *obligated* for the **care** of that *Guest/Consumer*, from the very beginning to the very end of the ***buying/owning*** process. But let's not forget the ***"Betterment Process"*** **never ends**, only ***evolves***!

It is now your turn, or as it is called, *"it's your up"*. I never particularly cared for this term, due to the fact that it *insinuates* that you are not fully aware, because you are evidently sitting down and need to get up and get ready to talk to somebody that's not a colleague. I refer to this as an *"obligatory commitment"*, or better yet… an *"opportunity"* (*"Opp"*)! *"It's your "opp'* (Opportunity for Success☺; Go figure!

"Opportunities" can arrive at any given moment, and that opportunity is a *Prospect/Consumer* ready to **buy/own**. Providing that they are in front of YOU, and you're ready to go with full awareness and your <u>open mind</u> is *intact*!

…Here is a prime example, and a great story of *inexpertness*. I am sure you're familiar with the name "Zig Ziglar", if not, I strongly advise to "Google" his name and research his books. In his book, ***"Secrets of Closing the Sale"***, he tells of an experience he had when his daughter graduated from high school, he was to take her to look at cars (*"buy a car"*) for her graduation present. On this particular day, with his daughter all dolled-up, as if going to the prom or a night on the town. Well, this father and daughter team wander into a local dealership, and don't forget the daughter is dressed to the hilt and glowing with excitement, being that *"this is the day she gets a new car!"* ...Why one might ask, do I indicate in parenthesis, (*"buy a car"*)?

Think about it...if it was your daughter and you have the clout as good ole "Ziggy", not to mention the scenario that has been created. All one has to do is simply "Land" the daughter, she is already *"emotionally involved"*, and wants a new car, and has *good/<u>Right</u>* **"Reason"**! Trust me "daddy" will comply.

Anyways, back to the story...As Mr. Ziglar and his soon to be a **"new car owner"** daughter arrive at the "Dealership" that sells the most cars of which interests them. They are eventually greeted by a salesman with a friendly and charitable demeanor, by asking... *"can I help you"?*, and Mr. Ziglar indicates to this so called "salesman", that his daughter has just graduated from high school and that they were interested in looking at cars for her graduation <u>present</u>. To Mr. Ziglar's *disconcertment,* of which I would consider a clerk, and not a salesperson, politely complies with a response for them to feel free and look around, and if they were to see anything they would like to let him know...

Now this clerk could have simply asked this **"prospect/buyer"** without thought or consideration of the direction he was to lead them, or is it, not to lead them, in the case of this clerk's non-assistance? *"Are you looking to look, or are you looking to buy?"* To my dismay, I have actually heard salespeople ask this *insensitive* and *unprofessional* question.

Procedure 3 — Greet & Meet

If YOU are a true professional at what YOU are doing, or are choosing to do for a living, your gifted *"radar senses"* would have targeted in on this *"prospect's/consumer's"* earnest interest to **"BUY"**, which he would then become a *"lay-down"* (guaranteed sale, easy money)!

…Back to the story of good ole Ziggy, and daughter's buying experience. Dealership #1 was definitely not number one. **No sale**. Off to Dealership #2.

How sad is this? These now considered *"lay-downs"* are greeted and treated the same way as they were at the first Dealership, except, as Mr. Ziglar states, *"this salesperson had B.O."*. **NO sale!** Dealership #3, just as bad, if not worse than the first two Dealerships. **No sale!** Get this, Dealership #4, the Ziglars got lucky. They were actually able to **buy** a car (**SOLD**)! Due to the fact, that the daughter once upon a time, dated the salesman… Now, how lucky is that, for both the Ziglars and the salesman. "Lay-Down"!

Now let's check your *'awareness skills'* regarding Zig's car buying experience. First, put yourself in the first salesperson's position as the Ziglars pull up and get out of their car, what is your first observation? Think about it…Being Zig Ziglar, I'm sure they got out of a nice car, indicating that they probably weren't hard breast, but well to do.

Second; the daughter was dressed to the hilt as indicated by good old Ziggy, which is a way that most people would not dress to merely go look at cars. Now, as a reminder note; as the old adage goes…*" you can't judge a book by its cover, so be careful or cautious!"* More on this topic in a moment…

It became more evident why his daughter was all dressed-up, once Mr. Ziglar mentioned the *'Reason/Purpose'* that they were there…*"to look at cars for his daughter's graduation present"*!

Now, how is your *'awareness observation'*? Is it a well to do man's daughter's graduation present, or is it a looking expedition to merely get information? In this type of scenario, one does not look at presents, they get presents. What a grand **"Opportunity"** for any "Salesperson" that has that **"What's Right"** mind-set!

Here's a perfect example of the perfect "mind-set; First, if You *"judge a book by its cover"*, YOU might be greeted back with a very negative response, that is if they were even greeted at all, or maybe do the opposite, and decide that YOU may be barking up the wrong tree so to speak and spinning your wheels. Where valuable time may be wasted. This is why it is so *imperative* to do a thorough *investigation/questioning* to determine who it is that YOU have the **Opportunity to Meet** and **Serve**! If this is not *properly* and *accurately* initiated, You will not and cannot know who it really is in front of YOU and why, until YOU *investigate* the situation at hand!

Here's a brief story and prime example of why it is very *imperative* not to *prejudge* your *Guest/Prospect*, whether it be in person or any other form of *communication*.

"Very early on, and at the very beginning of my journey to become a Professional Sales Mentor/Trainer…it was the late 70's and I was working with my first large ticket sales item (Bedroom Furniture)., of which waterbeds were one of our specialties and a hot ticket item for the times. On this particular day a kid in his early teens strolls in with skateboard in hand and starts looking around and pushing on the waterbeds, watching the waves go back and forth. At this point no one was eager to talk to this young fellow, being that he appeared to be merely a youngster on a hot summer day in Phoenix with nothing to do but pass the time skateboarding and pushing on waterbeds appeasing his curiosities. Well, I was a little green behind the ears myself, and figured I would pass the time and talk to this kid, and at the same time practice my pitch/presentation, if nothing else. Besides, I was

Procedure 3 — Greet & Meet

confident to believe that the kid has parents, and I was guessing that they could afford what this kid may want to own. Here comes the bomb…the kid was a paperboy and had saved up to buy/own what he wanted to possess alright, and that was a waterbed. He pulls out of his pocket a wad of bills, $387.00 to be exact, in small bills!"

Lay-down/Easy-sale! Bear in mind this was forty plus years ago. What would that $387.00 buy you today?

I'm willing to bet that this kid grew up to be a very successful individual…

Think about it!!!

He went after what he desired and **<u>accomplished</u>** it with **"Great Success"!**

Here's my point…

By being fully aware of not only who YOU are and where YOU are going, but just as important, coming to the *rationalization* and *acceptance* as fact , that at the very beginning of the *"Greet & Meet"* process, that it first has to take place, and that YOU are there to **<u>satisfy</u>** every *Guest's/Consumer's inquisitions* and or *Requisitions* to everyone's **"Complete Satisfaction"** (*The soon to be Customer, The Company, and You*), and every time YOU put yourself in the position to meet someone in a *"face-to-face"* or *"one-on-one"* scenario, it is your **<u>full responsibility</u>** to Satisfy the task at hand with your grand **"Opportunity"**!

"Opportunity"

OK, it is now your *"opportunity"* (OPP) to be a **success**, and time for your *awareness* to kick in. YOU should be <u>ready</u> and <u>alert</u> before the *Prospect/Consumer* even walks through the door, or in some cases, before they even get out of their car. If it is a pull up and park scenario where they are in the market for a new car let's say, notice the type of car they are currently driving, the condition it is in, their parking demeanor...where they park, how they park, etc. Notice any particular *'characteristics'* that may tell you something about this person, i.e. roof/ski racks, bumper/window stickers, personal license plates, any other type of license plate that may indicate personal preferences, which opens the door for *associated* or *in-common* conversation. This *'**astute awareness**'*, with *'**enthusiasm**'*, will greatly enhance your ***"Greet & Meet"!***

This will also give you very *'pertinent information'* about the **"personal character"**, and or **personality** of this *Guest/Consumer* (opportunity). Also notice how many people are in the car. What is their demeanor, such as facial expressions, facial direction etc...Is it conversational with another person, or are they gazing in a particular direction, maybe indicating a specific interest in something in particular? As they get settled in their parking spot, **do not,** I repeat, do not rush them, or things, especially your approach.

Wait until they are completely out of the car, and at that time, from a distance be *jovial* and *friendly,* **smile**, be sincere and **likeable**...interested in them as if a *"GUEST"* in your own home. Show *respect, compassion,* and *appreciation* in your *demeanor*. Don't be sloppy or lackadaisical in your approach, walk straight up with *confidence*. Be aware that YOU are not over boisterous (*animated* or *over excited*). Do not come across as a "robot" or being scripted, but most importantly, do not show *arrogance*. Only a *"Consumer/Customer"* has that *"Right"*.

Another *significant* thing to be *aware* of (*'significant awareness'*), is that just as YOU are processing the *Prospect/Consumer,* the *Prospect/Consumer* is also processing YOU. So, take your time, nobody likes being rushed. There is a *space/distance* that exists for every one individual, and that *"space"* or area should not be impeded upon with-out complete discretion…this space has been termed as *"Give me some space", "This is my space", "I just need a little space"*, etc. I like to refer to this as a *"Comfort Zone"*, and everybody has one.

By implementing this astute and *significant awareness* indicates that a *"Management Process"* is required, therefore, always respect your *Guest's/Consumer's* space and manage your awareness and be focused on YOU first! Ensure that YOU are **warm**, **friendly**, **patient**, and most importantly, **authentic**!

Another point to consider is the '*state of aura*' that may exist not only in yourself but just as important, the aura that exists in and around your *Guest/Consumer*.

If by chance you are not familiar with the definitive term for *"aura"*, allow me to be of assistance (not may I help you), some may even say… *" allow me to indulge you"*.

The definitive term for "Aura"; '*is a distinctive atmospheric quality surrounding any given source, or an energy field that is emitted from any living being'*… *"Opportunity/Prospect/Consumer/ Customer"*!

When the *"Greet & Meet"* approach begins, it must be *cool, calm, collected,* and most importantly, professional. As long as your awareness is truly in check, you will know what kind of *energy/aura* to exude. By utilizing the *'proper awareness'* you will be able to **mirror** the person in front of you more effectively. Here are some suggestions on how this can be accomplished…first, put into action everything that has been noted so far, and as you did early in the *"Greet & Meet"* process, observing your future *Customer/Customers* before they even put their feet on the pavement (blacktop), or as they walk through the front door.

As YOU are observing your *Guest/Consumer* from afar, again, do not enter *"their space"*! Which I will cover in further detail in the next segment. As you approach your new *opportunity* of **success**...The beginning of a new *"Relationship"*; from a distance, give them a *verbal greeting*, and stay *focused*, noticing their *demeanor* as you are approaching them. This is where *mirroring* begins (more on '*mirroring*' in a moment). YOU need to be observant of their reactions to your '*greeting*' from a short distance, and please, understand that this has to be the *first* thing that takes place upon greeting your newfound opportunity in order for YOU to acquire an effective '*Meeting*', and build an *efficient* and *effective* **Customer Relationship**! In other words, YOU have to establish your *"Personality Game Plan"* as You go! STAY *earnestly heartfelt* and one-step ahead of the game?

"Their Space"

What is construed as a *"person's space"*, and why are we so protective of that space?

With over 25 years of *"Greeting and Meeting"* people *face-to-face* on a professional level, I can confidently state as fact, that all people have *"Their Space"*, and they/we all have that *"Right"* to determine that space (*"Comfort Zone"*). This zone is usually about arm's length, stretched out in a circle about 3 feet. "Pretty simple", and just enough 'space' for a **"Handshake"**!

By establishing an early comprehension of **who** or how your guest may be by their demeanor, You are now properly prepared to *"Meet"* your grand opportunity '*face to face*' to complete your "**Greet & Meet**" approach!

You need to be able to read people *effectively* from the very beginning in order to move them along the *"Right Path"* to **"OWNERSHIP"**!!!

Being that everything has a beginning and an end, with the exception of *"Customer Relationships"*, and as we now know, **True Relations** never end, but only *prosper*! It is imperative to begin any relationship with an *"**open mind**"* full of *optimism* for a **successful** outcome, *"Checkmate"* if you will, or *"Closed Deal"*, earned *"Customer"*!

Think about when you first meet someone that you are interested in, don't YOU always *"put your best foot forward"* and present yourself with *confident* and *respectable* conduct, hoping for a *positive* and *acceptable reception*? When YOU are successful in your approach, YOU will then have a ***"Reception Connection"!***

"Connection"...

Now there's an interesting word that has a substantial amount of *significance* to the *"Sales"* and any other type of a *"Customer Relations"* process. To *"**connect**"* is to *'relate'*, to *'unite'*, to *'link together'*, creating a ***"bond"***!

When **"Relationships"** are listed as a *'main objective'*; That *"bond"* must be established as, and with a ***"Bond of Trust"!***

We are all very aware that *'first impressions'* are only a one time shot, but at the same time, somewhere in a naïve subconscious state, some have this *façade/notion* that there will be this grand opportunity to get a second chance at a *first impression*. One thing for certain is that, if there is to be anything to be taken advantage of, it is...

... "The First Impression"!

When observing the **Prospect/Consumer"** from a distance you will be given a *pro-active* head start of what type of a person (future *"Customer"*) you will be working for, and with. The distant verbal greeting is crucial...as you are approaching your new *"Opportunity"* for **success**...start your *"Greeting"* with a friendly and welcoming *attitude/demeanor* from a distance of at least 15 to 30 feet while verbalizing your *'jovial welcome'* proper *'inflection/tone'* in your voice while being fully aware that *"First Impressions"* can only be accomplished once and sets off a specific tone of how things may take place for the circumstances and or situation at hand (OPPORTUNITY)!

The same would apply if you were to be speaking with someone on the phone. Providing that You are well *tuned/honed'* in Your *'listening awareness'* skills, and this is another gift that we are all blessed with...the ability to actually listen and register, not only what is being said, but just as relevant, the tone of the one speaking at the other end. Sorry, I got off topic for a moment in regard to a *"Customer's Space"* ...

...This distance is determined by the original *"Comfort Zone"* (their space). The *'formula'* is computed by multiplying **_their space_** of 3 ft. x 5 or 10...This zone is called *"The Welcome Zone"*, which gives the *Guest/Consumer* a chance to feel **_welcomed_** and _respected_, without being rushed or crowded (*overwhelmed*).

In sales or any other *"Customer Relation's"* profession we have all heard the term *"Vulture"* ...someone who scavenges for prey ready to swoop down on and devour.

Please take note: *"Consumers/Customers"* (people) of all walks of life are also familiar with this term, which is why most people (*"Consumers/Customers"*) are somewhat *reluctant* to the point of rudeness when being approached by a Sales/Company Representative...So be *'cautiously aware'*, yet astute enough to know how YOU should *customize* your approach and give them *"Their Space"* so they can experience the aura of *comfort* and *wellbeing*! When this is accomplished, it becomes much easier to mirror the persons you are about to establish a bond and **_lasting relationship_** with!

"Mirroring"

Mirroring the *Prospect/Consumer* is when your awareness recognizes (*"Recognition Awareness"*) *body movements, facial expressions, reactions,* even *accents* or *dialects.* Copying the *"Consumer"* so to speak, by mirroring their demeanor and energy level. This form of mirroring is not to be construed as mimicking or copying your guest in a physical manner, but in an energy or personality format. This will strengthen and create *'Common Ground'* on a *personal* and *professional* level.

Be very careful when ***"mirroring"*** a *Guest/Prospect*. YOU do not want to come across as *patronizing, mocking, or condescending*, and worst of all, non-genuine. If you are skilled enough to utilize accents or dialects, take advantage of that ability, but be very subtle and cautious that you look the part and that you do not over emphasize or exaggerate!

Here's an example of what NOT to do…While working with a #1 Toyota dealership, there was a particular sales rep who had an appearance of being very Caucasian, actually Swedish in appearance with light skin, blonde hair and clean-shaven. He eventually grew a mustache and goat tee, and now appeared to be Swedish- German in appearance. Due to this new appearance, he acquired the nickname of Günter. One afternoon Günter was conversing with an elderly Hispanic couple while utilizing a very strong Hispanic accent that did not fit with whom these *Prospects/Consumers* were seeing across from them and conversing with, and unfortunately nor did it make sense to his *guests* and was taken as offensive… He lost the sale…although he did acquire a new nickname, "Günterrio."

Don't get me wrong, this method is very successful when used correctly, and although it may seem somewhat deceptive, it is for **Right Reason**!

The right reason is this... You have strangers in front of you that for some freak of nature reason, they may have none or very little trust, or simply a lack there of! It's that ring of confidence that has not been earned by whom they are allowing themselves to be in front of! When all YOU are simply trying to do is create and establish a *"**Relational Bond**"* on a personal level to assist your *guests/consumers* in a more proficient way to earn their business!! This process also establishes *"In Common Elements"* that enhances the *"**What's Right**"* process of *"**Betterment**"* to the **Customer's Benefit** for the long run!

These in common factors actually build <u>trust</u>, and <u>confidence</u>, which **strengthens** the *Customer-Representative "Relationship"* for *'**Continuous Growth**'* and **Success**. Just remember that YOU are not above them, and even though it's all about *"The Customer"* ...They are not above you either. Simply get on the same level, by establishing common ground by *"mirroring"* properly and <u>using</u> their **NAME**!

"What's in a Name?"

Once you have greeted and introduced yourself to your *Guest/Prospect/Consumer* and have exchanged names, be absolutely certain that you not only heard their name, but actually listened to it. Now throughout your entire communications with your *"Opportunity"*, be certain to use their *name/names*. This part of the process is probably one of the most important facets in establishing a <u>connection</u> toward **Customer Relationships!** The *"Name Process"* must be utilized on a consistent basis. Although, remembering names is not always easy. The easiest way to remember someone's name is by *'association'*, by associating their name with a name that you are familiar with.

Here's a good example of how "association' can work in remembering or establishing a *"Name Presence'*...Being a "Certified Chef" by trade, I eventually took the challenge to open a restaurant. Other than deciding what to serve up to the public, a 'name' also had to be chosen. So what does a new restaurant need to succeed other than good food, and of course "people" to eat your food. Well people don't pull up in buses or come in droves. Unless the food really is that good. Even though that may be a restaurant owner's dream. People have to know about the restaurant, and every restaurant has to have a name, so they know what to call it. When the restaurant is "new"; what do you do to get people to notice and remember your new restaurant when they haven't even tried the food yet? Come up with not only a catchy name but create a name association than will attach to their memory bank. So, what did I come up with for a name YOU might be curious enough to know, being new and what is it that a person associates with when you're new in the public eye.

Utilize some of the 'senses', speaking of 'eyes. I chose that one (eyes)...*imaging*! By focusing on imaging, I knew I had to create an **'*association*'** with the name and an image that would associate with one another. I knew what I was going to specialize in, and that was Chicken and New Mexico Chile'. The name of the restaurant became *"Chicken n' Chile's*, and Logo became a cartoon caricature of a chicken wearing a red chef apron and chefs bonnet while caring a cooking utensil in one wing and a burlap bag filled with red and green chile' thrown over its shoulder on the other, red and green chilies flying out of the tears in the bottom of the burlap bag while giving the impression that it was moving forward. Now people that would see the Logo would associate the image with the name… *"Chicken n' Chile's*

Very important; if you forget someone's name, it is not necessarily unprofessional or inconsiderate to smoothly ask them to repeat it. After all we are only human, although this can only take place once, because they have already given you their name once, and now twice. **Do Not** ask them the third time. This will indicate that you simply are not listening or rudely do not care, and may have the *'wrong motives'* in mind, which will be interpreted as an insult. If this takes place, you will probably get something like *"don't worry about it, just show me what you have to offer"*, and this will usually lead to a path of failure from the get-go. ..I'll discuss the importance of **'Paths' and 'Trails'** in Procedure 7 "Making it Happen *and Closing the Deal"*.

People like to hear their name...it all started when we were growing up as children. As children, our name was one of the first things that we associated with, or experience that was directly connected to oneself, other than mom and dad, but our name belonged to us, the first thing that was truly our own, and when we heard it, it was usually to our *"benefit"*, *("your name"..."it's time for dinner", "your name"..."it's time to come in out of the dark", "your name" ..."are you OK", etc.)* unless you were called by your first and middle name, this was usually not a good thing. When you get someone's name **"USE IT"** No one likes being called "Hey you". Sounds pretty impersonal doesn't it, and what's the *"benefit"* in that?

"Benefit"

Let's discuss **benefit**. Are benefits good or bad? ... To benefit is to *'have an advantage of'*, or to *'profit from'*, *'to assist"*, *'help'*, or *'do good to'*. We have been processed to connect our name with positivity and growth and unfortunately to our own *'benefit'*.

So what does this tell us? We have all been trained (processed) to be somewhat self-centered, and that directs us to wanting things that are to our benefit. When one is self-centered...the "focus" is on the wrong *"objective"* ... "YOURSELF"! Now I understand that one has to take *care* of one's *self*, but please be aware of the fact that there is a big difference between *'Self-Care'* and *'Self-Core'*, although they both exist in one's self...*"Self-Core"* relates to an awareness of doing *"What's Right"* for the *'benefit'* of others...where *"Self-Care"* on the other hand, only wants to *benefit* one's own self. When you *"Benefit The Customer"* ...Everyone Benefits!!! Can you see what I am saying? It doesn't even require eyes, but I will express to you what does, and that is '*eye-contact*'!

"Eye Contact"

When involved with a *Guest/Consumer* and future *Customer*, always present everything to *"their benefit"*. This is only accomplished when utilizing your *'full awareness'* and underlining of what their needs, wants and even hopes that they may have. Which requires an *"Open mind"*, a *"Positive Mental Attitude"* (PMA), and *'Eye to Eye'* contact. This PMA is all about the "The **Customer's Complete Satisfaction**", and them experiencing a feeling of authentic *'significance'* and *'appreciation'*. When someone can see your eyes, it indicates that you are being *'sincere'* and that YOU are *'genuinely interested'* in **their concerns**, and **their interest**, as well as the importance or implication of what you are stating. One thing that I have seen way too often outside on the black top during the day, is sunglasses being worn by company representatives while communicating with a guest, and this is a contradiction in terms.

One cannot *communicate* properly when the person that you are communicating with cannot see your eyes. After all, *"eyes"* are the *"windows to your soul"*, so they say. If you're looking at your feet and not in Your Guest/*Consumer's* eyes, **soul** brings on a whole new meaning, and becomes sole! And to mention, that if this is the case, the *"Window to Your Sole"*, will surely break as soon as You take the *'wrong'* step and not the *"Right One"*!

Eye contact is another important characteristic to doing *"What's Right"* in YOU. If someone can't see the whites of your eyes, how do they know you're being sincere about your intentions? If nothing else, every time an important point is made, make sure they can see your eyes. If you wear sunglasses, simply tilt them downward on your nose and respectfully peer over your glasses when presenting an earnest position about your product and or service. Trust me, this little gesture will be noticed and will strengthen the *"Relationship Development Process"*. Another little gesture or *"Natural Sense"* that generates strength in the *"relationship building process"*, is the *"sense of touch"*.

"Touch"

"Touch" can be a very *personal* subject to most anyone, although *'touch'* or *'human contact'* should never be given, nor taken in vain, but rather be *recognized* as one of the (5) five senses, and a deportment of *'contact'* to enhance *'connectivity'*. After all when you first *"meet-up"* with someone or are in a *'reception'* type scenario, what is the first thing we do?..."Shake Hands" or *"Embrace"* in a cordial hug. Now days, a *"high-five"* or *"knuckle-bump"*, even a *"shoulder slide"* seem to be the norm, generationally speaking. As long as you never stoop so low that you knee knock! Nobody likes a knee knocker! That's hitting below the belt! This a perfect indication that *"touch"* is an essential element to *"Human Behavior"*, which not only becomes an **important facet** to this *"Betterment Process"*, but also

establishes the <u>fact</u> that **"Touch"** is a requirement to succeed in **"Relationship Creation"** ..." *a gentle touch", "just a touch", "the golden touch", "touch of class"*, etc.

When working with a *Guest/Consumer*, don't be *intimidated* to tap that **person** on the shoulder in a friendly gesture to bring their attention to something of *relevance*, or a maybe a complimentary *"pat on the back"*, or once again, now days... a *high five* or a *knuckle bump*. As long as it works in generating a *"Representative/Customer"* **<u>bond</u>**...and it will!

What's Right
*Doing it For "The Opportunity"
Not to, "The Opportunity"*

Procedure 4
Fact Finding
*For
"The Customer"
"Relationship Building"*

We're gaining momentum, are you still with me? Is your attitude **"Right"**? Is your *'awareness radar'* **focused**? Are you well rested, fully charged and ready to **succeed**? Now...Do you get my point? You must be prepared from top to bottom, from the beginning to the *'completion/close'* of the sale. Notice that I did not say to the end of the sale, because a sale does not end, it is **achieved**! Only the **"Sale's Process"** has been completed, or a term I prefer to use; **consummated**! **EARNED BUSINESS**!!!

Here is irony for you, the answers to all the above questions maybe an absolute "Yes", but there will be no *"completion of the sale"* (achievement), if you are not in *complete acceptance* that everything YOU do or ask is <u>for</u>" The **Customer"**, and it is your accountability that this **process** depends on. Get the facts (*information, details, "the whole story"*). Ensure that you collect all the data to do...

"What's Right" For "The Customer".

As YOU begin the *fact finding* process your *awareness/alertness* is critical, for YOU have to be **spot-on** in doing **"What's Right"** toward <u>Your direction</u> of *"The Close"* of the sale, or achieving *"Complete Satisfaction"* for *"The Customer"* if YOU are in a *Customer Care* or *Customer Relations* **profession** where all a *Customer/Person* truly wants, is to be listened to and treated with **Respect** with a *resolution* to their *concerned inquiry* and or problem. For any Company we all know **The Bottom Line** is truly the *main objective* here; not just for Your employer, but YES..." *The Customer*".

What does this mean *"outside of this box"* ...Hold on we're going for a ride...Notice I did not say <u>in the</u> direction toward... **"Your direction"** was indicated, because you are at the helm and fully *responsible* to <u>direct</u> and <u>guide</u> your *guest,* the **Consumer/Prospect**, from the *"happy beginning"* of Your initial approach.

That's right, once again, each time YOU *"Greet & Meet"* someone *"face to face"* in Your *profession*, it is the beginning of a *"Relationship"* that never ends, but merely increases, and is always a *"Fact Finding"* **progression/succession**. A *"chain reaction"* if you will, linking YOU to the *Consumer/Prospect* and them to your product and the company you represent, but most importantly, other **Customer's**. This is where *"word of mouth"* enters the picture, yet *"listen of ear"* is of the utmost significance here! Due to the fact that it all starts at the beginning with a simple *smile*, a *sincere hello*, a *warm handshake* a, *"nice to meet you"* with an *"Earnest Welcome"* …NOT a cold, "can I hep ya"?

Think about this…If you were approached by a stranger, and the first thing about of their mouth is an indication that you "need help", and if one is welcomed with a "can I hep ya"? It's not only very poor grammar, which solidifies the fact that this kind of a greeting is an extreme insult to that person ("The Guest"). Now, let's say it's a polite *"may I help you"* or *"how may I help you"*? This type of greeting, although polite and a charitable demeanor connotation, a *"Guest/Consumer"* does not need charity, although they may need assistance! So, simply be more selective in your grammar and state…"*how may I assist you*"? or *"how may I be of assistance"*? This type of grammar/verbiage selection falls under the category of **respect** and **appreciation**, and these are the (2) two main ingredients that are of the utmost importance for ***"Customer Retention"*** and a ***"Customer's Complete Satisfaction"***!

If your intentions were *"Right"* from the very beginning, *"fact finding"* is relatively a simple process as long as it is all about *The Customer*…First … **listen** to what is being said about THEIR *'needs', 'wants', 'desires',* or even *'ideas'*. Even if those ideas *'appear'* to be a little askew and have created a misunderstanding about what it is that You are representing.

Notice here that I indicated one of the *"Customer's Privileges"* was *ideas*, and that those ideas <u>maybe</u> a little askew…The two terms that **connect** here are <u>appear</u> and <u>maybe</u>. It is your responsibility to not only *"find the facts"*, but to understand and accept the fact that the facts that may be in question is of great importance to that individual (*Consumer*). Unfortunately, there are people out there that are "no it alls", or at least they think they are, and, Well they most certainly have that *"Right"* if they fall into *"The Customer"* category.

It is entirely up to the true Professional to level things out, not straighten *"The Consumer/Customer* out! This means that YOU are responsible for ensuring that the *Guest/Consumer* is informed and guided in the correct and **Right** direction of their inquisitions. If they must be corrected! Simply, *'validate'* with complete ***concern*** and ***integrity***!

DO NOT create a negative *aura* (*environment*) from the very beginning or at any other time throughout *"The Process"*. As we all know, or have at least heard… *"ATTITUDE is EVERYTHING"*, and it goes both ways. It is your <u>*responsibility, aptitude, personality,*</u> and <u>*integrity*</u> to not only find the facts, but the *"Right Facts"* and do your absolute best to ***"Benefit The Customer"*** with a <u>Great</u> *"What's Right"* in YOU *attitude*…this does not merely mean having a vast knowledge of the product and inventory that you are peddling, but most importantly, fully understanding and guiding your *"Guest"* in the direction toward <u>their</u> *Happiness/Contentment*, and ***"Complete Satisfaction"*!**

As you attentively ***listen*** to your *Guest/Prospect/Consumer*, do not merely hear what they are saying, watch their ***<u>facial expressions, body language, responses</u>***, and or ***<u>reactions</u>*** to where you are leading them based on Your *"fact finding process"* and *technique*…that's Right, ***"<u>YOUR</u>"*** process. It's all on **YOU** to do the *"Right Thing"*, and to not only show off your esteemed *qualities* and *gifts,* but to **take action** and do **"What's Right"** for the **Consumer/Customer** and **"The Company"** that put their dependency and **"Trust in YOU"**, not your ego!

"Ego"

Now this segues into an entirely different topic..."**Ego**"...You have to *trust* in yourself to **"Do the Right Thing"** for **"The Right Reason"**, without inviting *"Ego"* to the party...Let's discuss *"Ego"* for a moment...Some say "ego" is good, some say "ego" is bad, so let's define "ego" as defined in the "New World Dictionary of America"... Ego is defined as... 1. *"the self"; "the individual as one self-aware of one's self"*. Unfortunately, with this type of definition it creates... 2. egotism and conceit.

There is another definition that will put everything in the *"Right Perspective"* that will knock your socks off, that is if you're wearing any socks, anyways I'll get to that in a moment...

First, let's break down conceit by simply using the first *synonym; "Self Importance"*. This right away or should I say, *"Not Right Way"* ...sends one's self in the wrong direction of *'success continuance'*. Some think they have it *"Right"* by bragging on themselves about what they did to a **Consumer** and now a **Customer**, instead of what they **did for** *"The Customer"* ...This my friend and future *victor*, is a detriment to this **"Betterment Process"**. ...This is *'conceit'*. I call it dragging, instead of bragging, because it drags on and on and on, when one should be bragging about their *'accomplished performance'*, of how they fulfilled a complete order by obtaining all the *'Pertinent Facts'* to... **"The Customer's Complete Satisfaction!**

Here is a *'simple'* example of the difference between *'conceit'* and *'confidence'*...conceit is when YOU think, YOU have it *"right"*, and *'Confidence'* is when YOU **Know** YOU have it *"Right"*. Pretty *simple* huh? And to be honest with yourself! Simplicity is the Key…read on!

…Back to the definition that I earlier mentioned that will put it all in the *"Right Perspective"*… ego; 3. Psychoanalysis: *'that part of the psyche which experiences the external world, or reality, through the senses, organizes the thought process rationally, and governs action: it mediates between the impulses of the id, the demands of the environment, and the standards of the super ego'*… what does this all sum up to? An illusion of "the ego"? *Stay 'aware'* and *'true to you'* to do… *"What's Right" in You*, for **ALL** involved!!!

Now that we have everything in a *proper perspective* and heading the *"The Right"* direction to get the *"Right Facts"* for the *"Right Reason"*, it's time to continue honing your craft toward *'continued success'*! As previously mentioned about a *Customer's* ideas appearing or maybe being a little askew. Do not *offend* but defend your allies (*The Customer*). Respect their views and understand that their ideas/views may have substance. Use this to your advantage.

Maybe their ideas are not out of line, but merely misinformed. Which would then put them out of kilter, and that is where YOU come into importance for a successful outcome.

"Fact Finding" is the main glue that adheres everything together when done correctly and for" Right *Reason"*. Like pieces in a puzzle… *"The Facts"* are what gives your presentation and demonstration validity and true meaning! YOU cannot complete a puzzle successfully if you don't have ALL the *'Right Pieces'* to put in the *'Right Place'*.

Listen to what matters to *"The Consumer"*, and at the same time ask the *'Right Questions'* at the *'Right Time.* This can only be accomplished by listening attentively to what truly matters and has *'realistic benefit'* to the *Guest/Consumer*. Speaking of *'realistic benefit'*...let's discuss that for a moment, and its value.

In order to present **'*realistic benefit*'** <u>effectively</u> and <u>efficiently</u>, you not only have to study and acquire the knowledge of your own product and company, but just as importantly, you also need to have proper knowledge of what your competition is all about and what they have going on, and I am not simply implying only what kind of promotion or sale that they are advertising at any particular time. It is much more complicated than that. You also have to acquire the knowledge of the product and have that knowledge always readily available in your ammunition belt to use to your advantage. This acquired knowledge must be near equivalent to the product that YOU are representing and selling. Once this is accomplished with great success, YOU will then possess the *accuracy* and *means* to be confident, not only in yourself, but also in your **'*Fact Finding*"** and **"*Landing*"** process. You will also have a greater confidence in your sales *delivery* and *presentation* of what or who it is that you represent. Which is YOU and the *"Company"* that employs YOU!

In *Procedure 5,* I will discuss in further detail about not only the significance of having knowledge of your *competition,* and what they are up to or selling, but also how you can actually prevent your prospect "Buyer" from ever even going to your *competition,* and it's *"The Consumer"* that makes that decision!

"Be a Detective"

Put yourself in the shoes of a detective as you grasp this part of the **"*Betterment Process"*** of doing **"*What's Right*"**. A detective's job is to *detect* or *interrogate* the subject at hand and get **<u>All the Facts</u>** with *validity* and *certainty*! This can only be achieved by asking all the *"Right Questions"* at the *"Right Time"* to get you to the *"Right Close"* ...

Not closure!

Here is a perfect depiction of true detective work portrayed by actor Peter Falk as "Lieutenant Frank Columbo" in a television series that was created in 1968 and ran through the 70's, you may recall it, if not I strongly advise to Google... "Columbo", as he portrays a humble yet disingenuous character, although he is always one step ahead of the *perpetrator* (*"Customer"*), always giving the impression that it is they that have the upper hand. He always leads the culprit in a way that they give themselves away by incriminating themselves to a self-confession or *"closes"* the deal himself, just as YOU will soon be doing. Remember that ALL *Consumers* are guilty of is to **buy/own** whatever it is that YOU are selling! This is why they or we are all called *"Consumers"* ...We like to "Consume" and or "Possess" things!!

You just have to be *"Open-minded"* enough and well-focused as YOU detect the *Guest/Consumer's* '*Emotional Intrigue*' and be aware of the Consumer's *buying/owning* *"Hot Buttons"* that need to be pushed, but not forced! Let's not forget that *"You can do it"* just as well as any detective. All YOU have to do is apply what is already *"in YOU"*!

What about these *"Hot Buttons"*, and what are they, and how do you know if it's a button to push or not? One may be inquisitive enough to ask! Well, here we go...

"Hot Buttons"

Anything that <u>interests</u> or <u>intrigues</u> your *Guest/Prospect/Consumer* and soon to be *"Customer/Owner"* of whatever it is that YOU may be presenting at any given moment is construed as a **"Hot Button"**.

As YOU probe the soon to be ***"Customer"*** for *'vital information'* (buying signals), take advantage of every moment that takes place, as well as every *response* and or *reaction* that YOU subject your *Guest/Consumer* to. Always be aware of your soon to be Owner's **"Hot Buttons"**. Be *astute* at all times to *ensure* that YOU do not miss a *'commitment/opportunity'*! Which in turn will go full-circle and segue into "***emotional commitments***"!

Once YOU push a **"Hot Button"**, *act* and *expand* on it by indicating or suggesting that whatever it was that YOU noticed, or what it was that piqued their *interest*, and how it seems or will be very <u>beneficial</u> to them, but **"*word'*** it in a way that seems to be <u>their idea</u>.

Always *present* your *questioning* in the *direction* of the *response* that YOU <u>need</u> at the time to *strengthen* and maintain a **<u>forward momentum</u>** to the final **YES!** The easiest way to the *"Final Yes"* is to keep your questions in the *yes* category, and by utilizing body movements in a *jovial* and *positive* manner. Keep your head nodding up and down while YOU ask the question (*tie-down question*), anticipating the **"*yes*"**. By exercising this *technique and* having an *'accurate focus'* on the **"Buying Signals"** (Hot Buttons), YOU can be <u>assured</u> that YOU will get a **"*yes"*** every time!

For example…

…"Mr. Customer I couldn't help but notice that as you were getting in the driver's seat you seemed to feel right at home by the way you took control and got yourself settled in and ready to go…It sure sits comfortably, doesn't it?" (while nodding your head up and down).

Observing, and then stating as fact that an obvious transition/alteration was taking place to the Guest/Consumer's

satisfaction and then confirming it with a positive question and gesture, Once again to the Guest/Consumer's "**satisfaction**"!

NOTE: Make sure that this is what was taking place at the time.

This type of questioning or technique is used to "**tie-down**" "The Prospect" with "pre-ownership commitments" (also known as mini-commitments) that will intertwine them '**emotionally**' to whatever it is that YOU are "**Fact-Finding**" them about so that as YOU proceed to the "**Landing Process**", it becomes a lot more effective as YOU develop and customize your "**Presentation**" and or "**Demonstration**" along the path/trail toward the direction of "**earning**" your Guest/Prospect/Consumer's business. This means in your phrasing and grammar selection, as well as tone and infliction in your voice.

Don't forget the "**Multiple Choice**" form of questioning as well. This gives the Guest/Consumer a choice between doing it this way or that way, never a choice between doing or not doing, ensuring yourself of always getting a **positive answer** while creating your own hot buttons.

Here's another example using the same allegory as the latter…" Now, it sure sits comfortably doesn't it Mr. Customer, or do you think you need a little more headroom?"

Note, that prior to asking this type of "**mini tie-down multiple-choice question**", I already have observed what has just taken place, therefore I would already know the answer to my question, I just wanted to confirm it in the Consumer's/Prospect's mind and have him or her state it verbally in some form of "**positive agreement**" creating an ownership tie-down!

"**The Consumer**" is now in a "committed position", he/she has to either agree or choose the latter. Either way the

Procedure 4   Fact Finding

answer will be "**yes**", which would be a 'signal indication' of interest, as well as **'emotional involvement'**, henceforth establishing an 'emotional connection' toward **"ownership"**!

"Emotional Involvement" is very critical, not only in **"Fact-Finding"** but when **"Landing & Committing"** as well. This is accomplished by stating or asking things in a way that is personalized to their inquiries and 'noticeable interests'. Do not pass up an opportunity to move forward toward **earning their business at any given time throughout your selling process!**

Always be selective in choosing the proper **"words"** in your questioning, in a way that will create **positive** "mini commitments" to own, or to be satisfied with. These are construed as **"Trail Closes"** or "pre- closes". The **"ABC"** selling process...

"Always Be Closing"!

You may have noticed that I indicated above, "*Trail Close*"... more on that topic later!

What's Right
Doing it For "The Opportunity"
Not to, "The Opportunity"

Procedure 5
Landing and Committing
For The "Customer"
"Benefit"

Procedure 5   Landing and Committing

Now that we have all the **"*facts*"** in check and ready to **"Land"** the *"Prospect/Consumer*. What does **landing** a *"Consumer"* actually mean? Think of an airplane landing. Can an airplane *"land"* itself, well of course not, at least not safely or '*successfully*', not even in autopilot, it can fly in autopilot, but not **"land"**. An airplane must have a pilot to not only fly the plane, but to guide it as smooth as he can for a '*smooth landing*', fully **focused** and **aware** of not only the plane (*Guest/Consumer*) that he is **guiding**, and is in **"*full control"*** of, but more importantly, '*attentive*' of any situation that may impede a journey of **success**.

The pilot must remain in constant *communication* with radar towers and air traffic controllers ('*information providers*'). Why is this so important for a pilot to land an airplane efficiently, other than to keep his passengers safe…A pilot has a reputation to withhold as a *true* and *responsible professional* who also wants to fly another day.

Let's put this in '*perspective*' as in *"Landing a Customer"*, in comparison to landing an airplane…Just as a pilot has to be constantly aware of his surroundings and in *proper communication* with the *"information providers"* (*Guest/ Consumer*), so does a sales person.

We as Human Beings have been gifted with and bestow a natural *enrichment* to *intellectually* gather and register information that out-weighs by a long-shot any manmade radar tower, and these would be termed as *"information connectors"*, which are the (5) five senses. This means that we have natural *"information providers"* or a built-in radar tower…

One must constantly be aware of **all** the *surroundings* when **caring** for a Guest and future Customer that not only depends on your *professionalism*, but also the **proper direction**. In most cases *"The Consumer"* does not always know what they actually want, only ideas of what they may be

Procedure 5 — Landing and Committing

interested in. But do they want it, well the answer could be yes, providing that they have all their research completed and are *"Completely Satisfied"* with their progress, or merely a lay-down. One way or the other, if they want it, a *"desire of ownership"* has to be initiated and **_accomplished_**!

One thing for sure that a *"Consumer"* does not want, is to be *misled* or lied to. What they do want or *expect* is to be **_listened to_** and **_guided_** in the direction of a *"proper landing"*, and to *"__their satisfaction__"*. The irony here is in most cases, they aren't even sure what they want to be landed on. All they know for sure is that they want to be listened to and **_cared for_** in the *"Right Way"* that *appeases* them. This is where YOU have to be as astute as a pilot is and utilize all your *receptors* to **land** the *Consumer effectively* and *smoothly*, by paying full attention of their *responses,* and or *reactions.*

You would be appalled to know what some representatives do to themselves by not using all their *abilities* to pay '*proper attention*' to what a *"Consumer"* is actually indicating what their *interests* or *objectives* truly are. This could be the error of the *"director/administrator"* or '*administration,* for not implementing '*proper protocol'* from the very beginning.

I have seen it where a *representative* will spend hours with a *Guest/Consumer* jumping through hoops and getting nowhere fast, and only succeeding at that, (getting nowhere fast) and then walking the **_"prospective buyer"_** right off the lot or out the door, or should I say, "*wrong...out the door!*", and then standing there dumb founded wondering what the heck happened. Where it is actually what didn't happen...*no earned business*!

...Notice I did not say, ***"The Customer"*** when stating *"off the lot"* and *"out the door".* These representatives have negated the possibilities of the *'opportunity'* to turn this *Guest/Prospect* into **"BUYERS/OWNERS"**, therefore *"The*

Customer" never really existed. When in this type of scenario, a T.O is required for a better chance of earning the *Guest/Consumer's* <u>worth,</u> and that is their earned business!!!

NOTE: ***"The T.O. System"*** seems to be a thing of the past…more on that in a moment!!!

I have even seen it where a "Rep" will do a follow-up call to regenerate an *opportunity* and find that they have already made a purchase elsewhere, and that isn't even the appalling news. Through further conversation with this "hope and a dream", the "Rep" discovered that they purchased something totally different than what the "Rep" did gymnastics for hours on end while these *"prospective buyers"*, Get this, the buyer that bought elsewhere was landed and even demonstrated on a 4-door sedan and probably more than one. Here's the irony, the *"buyer", <u>now owner</u>* that bought elsewhere bought a 2-door truck, go figure. This is a prime example of how crucial it is to be on your toes and know your P's and Q's so to speak. In other words, find out what is really going on throughout your ***"fact finding"*** process!

It really is a disservice to everyone and everything involved…The *"Guest"*, the *"Company"*, the *"Product"*, the *"Numbers"*, the *"Relationship Opportunity"*, and yes, even YOU…when one spends all that time, energy, and effort to come up empty handed. It truly is a fiasco and a disservice to oneself! Something we all are aware of is *time, energy,* and *effort* are to be ***<u>invested in,</u>*** not wasted.

Here is an important tip for you… There is no such thing as a *"be back"*. Once this is fully understood and accepted that this is not a myth but a *"fact"*, you will have more astuteness in your *"landing process"*, and like *"first impressions"*, there are no second chances if you don't get it ***"Right"*** <u>the first time.</u>

Procedure 5 — Landing and Committing

The importance of doing a *"proper landing"* is due to the fact that in order to get the *"Prospect/Consumer"* **emotionally involved** and having a desire to *consume/possess*, they have to be *"in to win it"* …the actual product, not a prototype. This also means YOU my comrade in arms. They have to be able to get 4 of their 5 senses involved: *'Smell', 'Touch', 'Sight', and 'Sound'*. Which can only be established if your future *"Customer"* is *'**emotionally interested/involved**'*. With this involvement of interest, and all these *"Natural Senses"*, it is rather simple to get *"The Prospect"* emotionally involved for ownership... This is also where YOU can reasonably gain momentum toward the direction in getting your *Guest/Prospect/Consumer* and soon to be *Customer/Owner* to *"Emotionally Feel Ownership"* for your Product and or Service and have a greater amount of ***appreciation*** of YOU!

Always *'lead'* your *Guest/Consumer* in a *smooth, gradual,* and *steady* direction by spending extra time on particular subject matters that your *Guest/Consumer* may have. The more astute you are to **their** concerns and or *interests*, the easier it will be to make a smooth and *"accurate landing"* on that one item ***"they just can't live without"***! They evidently are already interested in your product and or service or they would not have put themselves in the position to allow you to be in their presence. Actually, it's allowing themselves to be in your presence, or maybe they're, *"just looking"* …Don't believe it…They are looking to buy, providing that there is a *"Viable Reason"* to do so and a ***"Professional and Self-Conscious Representative"*** to guide the way!

Here's an example…When I was in my mid-twenties, employed with a waterbed company called "United Bedrooms" in Phoenix AZ as their first manager in a growing company. At the time, to some, waterbeds were considered for hippies and such, although with a growing popularity and know how marketing, little did they know that the man behind this soon to be "household" name company in the Phoenix Metropolitan area, new how to *"getter done"*! His objective was to saturate the market with huge bedroom furniture showrooms and let the mass public know about it. Which we did with 7 established showrooms in 5 years...Well to make a long story short, one of the build to suit showrooms was designated in Mesa AZ and happened to be next door to a "Sizzlers" steak house, and right around dinner time "folks" would come in (folks was the term used in Mesa) to *"kick tires"* (pass the time).

I would refer to these types of looky-loos as *"tooth pickers"* instead of *"tire kickers"*, being that they were coming from a restaurant with toothpicks in their mouths. Well one evening these *"tooth pickers"* (*elderly married couple*) meander in with absolutely no intention to buy, not even shopping, so they stated... *"just looking"*. If anything, they were merely there to walk off the big meal they evidently just had and maybe settle some curiosities about waterbeds. Well, what better place to be than in a furniture store with lots of waterbeds and nice bedroom furniture to look at, especially for the wife. Notice my astuteness to notice that it was the wife that was enticed by what was being presented to her and hubby. By my *awareness* and *enthusiasm,* I was able to establish a level of *communication* by getting them to *"trust"* and *confide* in me. I focused on the wives' emotions, yet at the same time I was able to gain confidence from the husband. So much so that I had him laying down on one of the waterbeds, literally (*trust me they were no lay downs*).

As I was acquainting with the wife about the product and its *sleep-quality 'benefits'*. As I led her over to where her husband was recuperating from his big feast and had the wife lie next to her husband. I was able to get them so comfortable in a *"comfort zone of trust",* that I established a mood of solace relaxation to the position that I could lie next to either one of them and sell the product of sleep, to their **"health benefit"**. Not only did I achieve a *"Relational Bond"* with these two *"looky-loos/tooth-pickers"* but was able to lead them to a grand **opportunity** of ownership benefitting themselves, as well as leading this *"opportunity"* to earned business for the Company on a complete bedroom set with a *'substantial gross'*...and yes, I benefited as well!

Now, that's what I'm talking about all along in this *"Betterment Process"* of doing *"What's Right"* ...ALL come out WINNERS!!

What is the moral of this story...Establish the *"get in bed"* with your *"Prospect and soon to be a Customer"* kind of **TRUST**! Metaphorically speaking!

It is entirely your *'responsibility'* to level things out so you're not dealing with a *"Distant Buyer"*. Now, I just indicated a *"distant buyer"*, but I did not indicate what type of *distance*. Are they going to make a decision in the distant future? Or are you **not connecting**, and this is creating a distance between you and your *"Prospective Buyer?*

One thing for certain, you don't want your *"distant buyer"* to buy at a distance across town at the competition!

An *"Effective Landing"* is crucial toward the direction of *"The Close"* or for a deal to ever be *'consummated'*, for this fact...would you spend a lot of your *time* and *effort* to **"buy"** (*spend your hard-earned money on*) something that you truly were not interested in owning? Probably not. Unless it was given to YOU. YOU might then consider owning it, *"You wouldn't look a gift horse in the mouth"*; so to speak, but would YOU consider it a satisfied deal if YOU were to pay your hard earned cash for it?

"Landing Effectively"

Here is how YOU **land effectively**...From the very beginning of your hello, your *'Astute Awareness'* and *'Progressive Connectivity"* should have begun regardless of what, or who it is that YOU are representing.

By learning and *implementing*, the **"What's Right"** process... YOU will have asked all the *'pertinent questions'* and have *observed* what it is, or why it is that your new *"guest"* is in front of YOU. ***"Tie-down Questions"*** are the best solution to validate the what's and what not's providing that they are related to your guests *inquisitions* and *requisitions*...Remember a ***"tie-down"*** question is where YOU ask a question that puts the soon to be *"Customer"* in the position where they are **committing** themselves in **agreement** with whatever it is that YOU have directed them to understand or believe about your product or ***their situation***, and or circumstances.

Note: Always in a positive nature with a **"YES"**, or an *elaboration* that defines exactly what it is that YOU and *"The Product/Service"* can and will do **"for them"**! Targeting this type of response will always lead YOU and the **"Prospect/Consumer"** toward the *"Positive Direction"* of **"Complete Satisfaction"** and earned business!

YOU are now ready to move your *Guest/Prospect* forward to the next level of *"Ownership' and* turning them into a *"**Customer**"* by *"Landing"* them on the **"Right"** item (*unit or situation/circumstances to their Complete Satisfaction*) ...and to be *"Right"*, is to be ...*" **EXACT"*** on what you and your *Guest/Prospect* agree on.

It is critical that YOU have it narrowed down to one single and ***exact*** item/issue or at least something that earnestly piques their interest. Based on your *analysis/investigation*, it should be something that resolves their inquiry or curiosity and would even consider owning before YOU head out on a Demonstration ("Demo"), or explanation or justification. Don't forget that your *guest/consumers* need to be **"emotionally involved"** if it is something that they are to *possess/own*! If it is a scenario from an existing *Customer*, and they are dissatisfied. They are probably already **"emotionally involved"**. Time to *investigate* and *determine*, "**what is really** *going on?"* It is completely up to YOU, and even to **"Your"** *'benefit'* by having your soon to be **"buyer/owner"** and or **"Completely Satisfied Customer"**!! Anyone **"Customer"** has to be <u>emotionally involved</u> in order to maintain a **"Committed Attitude"**, and that means...

"Loyalty and Retained Business"!

The best way to term this is...Say and do things that will get your soon to be *Customer* **"Psychologically Involved"** where <u>they</u> **emotionally** feel **ownership** for the product! When **"Landing"** or *determining* what the real *situation* is, and *understanding* that it is to...

<u>**"The Customer's Complete Satisfaction and That They Will Definitely Recommend!"**</u>

Let's take a step back for a moment...Remember the analogy of *"The Pilot"* landing a plane. Would YOU not be as *selective* as he, hoping, if not praying that **"The Landing"** is <u>"Spot-On"</u> to completion with **"Complete Satisfaction"**?

"Remember, it's a (2) two-way street", or is it a **"Runway"**?

Here's a demonstration of how involved and detailed one must be in order to get *"The Landing"* exactly **Right**...first, one has to be *judicious* enough to the extent of knowing **exactly** what it is about the *"The Product"* that will be *conducive* to your *"Guest"*, and then *"Conductively Connect"* YOU. Where then the three will connect in a divine unity (*You, the Product and The Customer*). If uncertain, there must be something that has not been revealed by or drilled-out of your *Guest/Prospect/Consumer*. If this is the case, it's now time for YOU to get *"emotionally involved"* for your *Guest/Prospect/Consumer* and assist in making decisions for them or use the **"T. O. System"** (more on the T.O. System in a moment). For at this point and time, your *opportunity* is merely a *"Guest"* looking around and not a soon to be **"Customer/Owner".**

As I previously mentioned, sometimes a *"Consumer"* does not themselves know exactly what it is that they want. Time to grab the *"bull by the horn"* and break it down to the ridiculous. How YOU might ask…pull out all the stops by making decisions for them yourself, by tangibly putting them in a *"Comparison Reality State of Mind"*, by showing competitive facts that prove beyond a shadow of a doubt that your product and or service is profoundly **superior** and worth ownership! **NOTE:** By some, this may be construed as badmouthing your competition, but as the next *"Procedure"* will verify, This is not the case at all, but only a benefit! I will explain in detail what it is that I am referring to as a benefit, not only for your future *"Customer"*, but just as importantly, the "Company" YOU represent, and yourself as well.

Here's an *'explanation'* and *reasoning* for a T.O….

"The T.O…" To **"T.O."** is to *"Turn Over"* the *Guest/Consumer* to another Sales Representative or Manager, creating a different opportunity to *"connect"*, where then another Representative will *"Take-Over"* the **"Opportunity"**.

The **"T.O. System"** has become somewhat *obsolete*, or not very common in today's Business Practices, which is a misfortune to not only *Companies* that are dependant on volume sales to achieve their '**Number Objectives**', but just as unfortunate, or misfortune for **"the opportunity"** to *acquire* another **"Customer"** from a Referral. This is why **"Customer Relationships"** are so **vitally important** to a **"Company's Long-Term Success"!** But, in order to have *authentic* and *long lasting* "Relationships" with your *"Customers"* …it's so much more than just *establishing common ground!* There has to be a **connection**, and not all can connect, or at least not for the **'Right Reason'**. Let me put this in a broader perspective...First one has to understand and accept the fact that the *"Customer"* is the *"**Reason**"* that an initial opportunity is bestowed upon YOU and or *"Company"*, not to mention the dollars that may have been *spent/invested* by *"The Company"* to get people in the door, creating such **opportunities**!

When it comes to following or establishing a **_path_** of non-resistance from your *Guest/Prospect/Consumer,* it enhances the road of **_opportunity_** toward establishing *"**Long-Lasting Relationships**"* with and for *"The Company"* of which You have been given the opportunity to work for and represent!

If YOU are unable to get your guest interested enough to get involved, and this means interested in YOU. Don't forget they don't know YOU, and more times than not, they don't want to know you. Here's the point...give them a chance to get to know YOU; Don't blow it from the very beginning, (*refer back to what YOU have understood thus far in this read!*). There's an old adage in the *"Profession"* of selling...and that is *"the sale is made with-in the first 30 seconds of the process"*, i.e. *"**The Greet and Meet Process**"*. If You are unable to establish some form of connection from the very beginning or merely cannot *"land"* them on a specific item that honestly '*compels*' their interest...It's time to **T.O.** before any more time has elapsed and the opportunity no longer has an interest or runs out of time!

Another time to **T.O.** is any time that YOU are losing control of the situation, and your momentum is diminishing along the *'path/trail'* to earning the *Guest/Prospect/Consumer's* **worth** (*business*)!

Note...this is where **_TEAM_**WORK and '*sacrificial successes* comes into play.

Here is an example ('*Reason*') why one would segue into a T.O., and yes, it is a segue and it must be smooth and seamless…meaning the **"*T.O. Process*"** must <u>*seem*</u> like a transition from one to another is natural, **to and for** the *'benefit'* of the *Guest/Prospect/Consumer*. Where the *Guest/Prospect/Consumer* will be <u>*less*</u> stressed and more content knowing that it is they that really matters, and it is ***their needs*** that hold ***top priority***, even to the point of the Sales Representative making a sacrifice, of which in most cases the *Guest/Prospect/Consumer* is not even aware that a sacrifice has been prearranged.

Here's the dilemma and what I have noticed and experienced with the three (3) major Automobile Dealerships (*Dodge, Toyota, and Lexus*) of which I have had the pleasure to work with, and learn from, and that is that the T.O. System is familiarized with, but not practiced unless the original sales person is not readily available for a fortunate "Be-Back"(*return of a soon to be Customer*), it is only then that a T.O. takes place to ensure that the *Guest/Prospect/Consumer* is ***taken care of*** and a sale is made.

Now this is where the **'*sacrifice*'** takes place if the pay *structure* is on a commission basis. A *"split deal"* is now warranted. This is where the original sales person now has to *sacrifice* half of his commission, and half of the unit/product count, which can effect his/her monthly sales figures, and even annual figures that are relevant to Factory and or Dealership bonuses, but there is a catch for these ***"annual bonuses"*** …and that is **"Customer Satisfaction Survey Percentages"** .

More details on this topic later in **"*Procedure 8 and the "The 7 R's"*.**

In brevity, let's discuss the subject matter of **TEAM**WORK and the "***significant value***" that it brings to the "*entire process*" of *acquiring* and *satisfying* a **"Prospect/Customer"**!

As for any *Company/Corporation*, *"**TEAM**WORK"* is the "***building-block***" and one of their *structured* ingredients to *attain* their objectives, yet, when you break it down to *'rational sense'*, *TEAMWORK* should be ***"The Foundation"***, and not merely a "building-block"!

Everyone wins when ***"TEAMWORK"*** is incorporated into the mix on a consistent basis...*Together Everyone Achieves More!!!*

Now, let's take Teamwork out of "The Box" of normal practices and thought patterns. This *'structured process'* goes two ways and full circle, and that is to ***"TEAM-UP"*** with whomever it is that YOU have been given the *honor* and *opportunity* to speak with or to be in front of! Another term that could be used is ***"Partner-Up"*** with your ***"Opportunity"***. As I mentioned moments ago...*Together Everyone Achieves More!!!*

Here's my point...When one is aware of and accepts as fact that when one T.O.'s a *Guest/Prospect/Opportunity*. Everyone come out a winner with this aspect of TEAMWORK...Therefore there really is no sacrifice providing a sale is earned and consummated to **Complete Satisfaction!**

Here's an example of a *"smooth"* T.O. ...

"Mr./Miss Customer (use their name), *I just came up with a great idea, hang on for a moment, I'll be right back!"* ...As You *'inform'* Your *Guest/Prospect/Opportunity* that YOU have a *"great idea"*, ensure that YOU are presenting this offering with *excitement*, indicating that your idea is to ***their benefit***!

...Now when You return, You are going to have someone else with You, whether it be a Manager or another Sales Rep, just be certain that whomever it is that YOU are T.O.ing to is **professional** and *astute* enough to *"Take Over"* the situation.

Once You return with the Calvary, make an introduction as such...

"*Mr./M.s Customer* (use their name), *this is so and so my Manager, the idea I had was that I felt that I wasn't answering all your questions adequately enough, and I wanted to make sure that all your inquiries were not only answered, but also that You're directed to the right way!*

What do You do now that your *Guest/Consumer* has been "***Taken-Over***" (T.O.) you may ask... "SHUT-UP" and listen! It is very <u>*imperative*</u> **Not to Speak**, for You do not know the direction of which the person that YOU just "*Turned **Over***" (T.O.) your *Guest/Prospect/Opportunity* to (*and I don't mean North, South, East, or West*) is going to lead them in. In other "words', establishing an '*emotional'* or *'personal'* "**connections'** and then have the advantage on this second chance to ascertain what it is that may "***Turn-On***" (T.O.) this *Guest/Consumer* so that they can be led along the <u>path</u> to "***Ownership***"!

I will give other examples of <u>**how**</u>, <u>**when**</u>...and, as we are now processing, <u>**why**</u> "**The T.O.**" ...in ***Procedure 7 "Making it Happen"***.

If by chance as YOU are reading along and taking this all in of which is already *"in You"*, and sitting there thinking...

" *Wait a minute I'm a "Pro" at what I'm doing, and I know what I'm doing, and always know where I'm at with <u>my</u> customers and what's going on. Why should I give up half and take a chance of being a half unit short to hit bonus level. Besides, I can get the whole deal at a later date when they come back and ask for me!"*

This is a Grand thought, and maybe even a great attitude to have, if YOU are only in it for a one time shot with the hopes of someone coming back for a second shot. What they are sincerely looking for when they are in front of YOU, is a

Procedure 5   Landing and Committing

"Grand Opportunity" to *"Buy/Own"*, so that they no longer have to go around hoping for a *"True Sales Person"* to end the agony of *"Looking"* and *"Shopping"* around going from one place to another. Let's not forget that they (*Guest/Prospect/Consumers*) would not be in front of YOU if they were not already interested in whatever it is that YOU are *representing* and *"SELLING"*! Which indicates that they are already somewhat...

"Emotionally Connected"!

Let's also not forget that everything goes *"Full Circle"*. You've heard it before... *"What comes around, goes around!"* Under these set of *circumstances*, YOU owe it to yourself to broaden Your vantage point, or should I say, *"Advantage Point"*, and step out of that particular *"Ego Box"!* There is absolutely nothing wrong with this *"sense-of- self"* worth and a *"Ring of Confidence"*, but one has to consider as "fact"...hold on to Your britches...These *"Guests/Prospects"* are not Your *"True Opportunity"*, *"They"* are the *"Opportunity"* of *"The Company"* or *"Organization"* that YOU have been given the *"Grand Opportunity"* to *Represent* and become an *"asset"* to and for their (*The Company*)

"Complete Satisfaction!"

On a final note, on this subject; consider this... **isn't a little bit of something better than a whole lot nothing?** Which, in this scenario of *"The Betterment Process"* of doing *"What's Right"* in You. YOU will have...absolutely nothing, if a *"Personal Connection"* is not established from the *"Hello/Welcome"* and *ensuring* that the *Guest/Consumer* is being directed in the proper direction to pique their *interest* and *enthusiasm*. If this is not established, You are then *"barking up the wrong tree"*! Trust me, YOU will get

Procedure 5 — Landing and Committing

<u>absolutely nothing</u> if YOU don't give the *"Guest/Prospect* "a second chance to ***"Connect"*** while there! Don't hold your breath waiting on a be-back! Where YOU are taking a chance to end with absolutely nothing! Now, *"Choice"* or *"Chance"* comes into play. Time to make a choice to keep the process going or take a chance (gamble) that they will return (be-back)! If you do by chance choose to depend on a be-back…have them, ask for Mr. or Ms. Blue. Because that is the color YOU will be turning while holding your breath waiting for their return!

What's Right
Doing it For "The Opportunity"
Not to, "The Opportunity"

Procedure 6
Presentation & Demonstration
For
"The Customer"

Procedure 6 Presentation & Demonstration

This is where the *"FUN"* really begins. Yes, I said *"Fun"* ...*fun is to enjoy, to have pleasure in, to be excited about, to be exuberant!* YOU don't have to be an *"actor"* and *pretend* that you are having a good time at what you're doing or *presenting*, and don't forget, *"it all starts with* YOU! Be authentic in all that YOU do. YOU don't have to be an *actor* to have fun! Think about that...if one has to: *act"* like they're having a *'good time'*, well what does that truly tell one's self... *"I'm really not having any fun"*, and if YOU know *yourself'* well enough, and I am sure YOU do. YOU know if you're not *enjoying* yourself, it's not going to turn out quite the way YOU originally had anticipated. So, where's the *Fun* and *success* in that?

Some people are just processed as actors. *"Actors"* are *performers, artists, players, or artiste*. Don't get me wrong...there's really nothing wrong with acting or being an actor. The question is...What kind of an actor are YOU?... Are YOU a *performer*, an *artist,* a *player,* or an *artiste*? Or are You a con, a *"one-time shooter"*, putting on a performance to merely play the game?

If YOU choose to be an "actor", **choose wisely**. If YOU like to *perform*, perform for the *"Right Reason"*. There are (2) two terms of **significance** here that should be **focused** on... (1); is to *'perform'* each *"Procedure"* with *"Satisfactory Completion"* and (2); to execute that *performance* not only to the *'benefit'* of Yourself and the Company, but for, here it comes...*"The Right Reason"*, which is ...*"THE CUSTOMER"!!!*

Or YOU can **choose** to *perform* with an *attitude* that emits a *"put-on"*, and that is not to be earnestly involved with the individual's real situation at hand, and maybe not even your own. Not knowing your product to its utmost potential, and not staying updated with your *competition*. Focusing on yourself, and not the *"main objective"*, and that's the *"Prospect/Consumer and soon to be Customer!"* As YOU

Procedure 6 — Presentation & Demonstration

strive to climb the ***"mountain of success"***, and as YOU ***"reach the top"*** of that mountain of success regardless of your *visions*, please take note... *"it is to look-out over into the world, not for the world to look-out and up at YOU."* That's *ego* once again crashing the party. In a nutshell... establish a *"side by side"* working foundation with your *Guest/Prospect/Consumer* and trust me, YOU <u>will</u> *"reach the top"*, **inevitably!**

I need to also elaborate on another component of *"acting"*, due the fact that it is not only OK to act, but it must be for the ***"Right Reason"***! When done so it *can* also be considered a *prerequisite* in the *process* of doing ***"What's Right"***! The **<u>reasoning</u>** behind being in an *"actor state of mind"* is due to the fact that as we all know, every situation and everyone is different with individual **<u>*'characteristics'*</u>** such as *personalities, moods,* and *desires.* This is where YOU have to be fully on your side, for *"The Opportunity"* ...by not only <u>knowing</u> your *"stuff"*, but also being able to *communicate* and *respond* and ***"lead effectively"***, not only in the way YOU <u>**present yourself**</u>, but how <u>spot-on</u> YOU are in your **<u>perceptions</u>** and the **<u>Strength</u>** in your... *"Product Demonstration"*!

Get a ***"grip-hold"*** of the reality that You are the '*Key Ingredient'* or *"Director"* of where the *Guest/Prospect/Consumer* is leading YOU! Sounds contradictory, doesn't it? Well, there's that *"full circle"* again!

Guest/Prospects/Consumers are the Producers, and You are the Director!

In the *"process of selling"* there is only <u>one ultimate</u> *"Goal"*, and that is to...

Procedure 6 — Presentation & Demonstration

"Close the Deal with 100% Complete Satisfaction"!

Getting to the *"Close"* is not always an easy task, unless one comes across a *"lay down"*, then that's a whole different story, yet still a great *opportunity*, but few and far between, especially this day and age with the variety of competition and the easy accessibility through the web and social networking, where everything is at the fingertips, and I mean literally.

In normal selling situations, it <u>requires</u> *strategy*, a *proficient* **"Game Plan"**, and not a '*stratagem*'. Like a ***chess game***, you cannot *trick* or *ruse* your way to a *"checkmate"*. <u>You must *plan* and *strategize* your way to **"Victory"**</u>!

I learned this early on as a kid by just merely playing the game of chess, but little did I know that this would be the beginning of a great career in *"Customer.*

Relations" and *"Communications"* that enables me to share these factual *experiences* and *successes*.

When I stepped into the profession of direct *"face-to-face"* selling with the company I previously mentioned, i.e. "United Bedrooms" ... which was in its infancy stage at this particular time; therefore there was a lot of idol time waiting for the front door bell to ring with the next *"happy-go-lucky"* prospect to enter. The man behind the company and I both just happened to enjoy the game of chess, which at the time, I thought it was a little odd to coincidently have a chess board conveniently and readily available right behind the counter. It was a pretty good size chess board, set upon a good-sized table with large chess pieces! Little did I know that this was to be part of my *training* and *honing* of a **"*skilled strategy*"** and *aptitude* of how to ***effectively manage***, not only your next move but actually be the ***front-runner*** and *direct* your opponent's next move. As well as the *perseverance* it takes to **"WIN"**! In the *"game of chess"*, you must always be at least

Procedure 6 — Presentation & Demonstration

one step ahead (*if not more*) of your *opponent*, focused on their <u>eyes</u>, their <u>actions</u> and <u>reactions</u> at all times, anticipating their next move before it ever occurs, by <u>choosing</u> your next move and selecting the <u>*"Right"*</u> men and where to move them and at what time...many choices to make, and since you want to <u>win the game</u> against this opponent, of whom is considered an adversary or challenger, They also have the same *objective* as YOU, and that is to walk away a <u>***winner***</u> of the game or *competition*.

Now let's do a *"paradigm shift"* to a **Consumer**...they most certainly are not your foe/enemy, but quite the contrary, **<u>they are your ally and union to success!</u>**

In the *"Game of Selling"*, it most certainly can be considered *"a game"*, although it's a game where everyone **"WINS"**! In fact, ...ALL are **"WINNERS"** as long as YOU are consistently aware of and do...

"What's Right"!

By this time in the process of doing *"What's Right"*, YOU should have a strong recollection and threshold of the direction of which we are proceeding in, and that is to be **<u>constantly aware</u>** of all that is **<u>pertinent</u>** to your soon to be **<u>Buyer/Owner</u>**...of

"Complete Satisfaction!"

At this point of any selling process *"***The Consumer***"*, same as YOU, have many *choices* to make and *decide* on, and it's up to YOU to simplify the **<u>Buying Process</u>**, and to make it an **<u>enjoyable experience</u>** for your *Guest/Consumer* as YOU guide them toward the *"***Ownership Process!***"* Make it as **"FUN"** and as *Comfortable* as YOU can, by simply indicating and *presenting* yourself as an individual that enjoys what they do and **<u>having fun</u>** doing it! *"Gettin' er done"*!

All YOU have to do is simply be *intuitive* enough to **incorporate** *diligence* with **sincere compassion** and an *"attentive ear"*. There is a technique termed…

"Covering an objection before it occurs"! Which pertains to the concept of chess, i.e.

"Anticipating the other player's next move" before they do. In other words, …

Overcoming an Objection <u>before</u> it occurs!

Providing that Your *Heart* is in the **"Right Place"** and Your *motives* are in check, YOU <u>can</u> and <u>will</u> be on top of your game, where YOU will be able to *calculate* and *deduce* your next move *accurately* and *succinctly*!

Here's where the **<u>FUN</u>** kicks in…" hold on we're putting it into overdrive"!

Simply put, in a quote by *"Henry David Thoreau"* (1817-1862) … *Thoreau;* a compilation of *"Quotes"*.

"Simple Science"

"When the mathematician would solve a difficult problem, he first frees the equation of all its encumbrances, and reduces it to its simplest terms. So simplify the problem, distinguish the necessary and the real. Probe the earth to see where <u>your</u> main roots run!"

Not only does this profound quote have *relevance* in the *"Life Process"*, it also **<u>unites</u>** in the process of **"What's Right"**…"By probing the *Consumer* to see where **"<u>their</u>"** main **Buying Roots** run…*("Hot Buttons"),* as well as the roots within Yourself!

<u>**"Keep it Trouble-free and Uncomplicated"!**</u> …

It's time to do a **<u>"Presentation"</u>** …" Buckle-Up"!

"The Presentation"

Now that it is *confirmed* what it is that your very soon to be *"Buyer/Owner";* and what it is they will soon *"**Own**",* YOU can now get into more *detail* about what it is that they, at this point should be somewhat *"enthusiastically excited"* about, and YOU should also have established their full *"**trust**"* and anything that YOU state or *demonstrate* to your *Guest/Prospect* will be taken with *strict confidence!* Ensure that YOU get your future *Customer* not only *"emotionally involved",* but just as *vital,* get them *__involved__* in any way possible, as long as they appear to be enjoying themselves, or at least seem comfortable with your *directives*! Sometimes YOU just have to *instigate* the fun yourself. Don't be hesitant to make them laugh…this brings not only a smile to their face, but also creates *"Happy Thought Patterns"*!

For example…referring back to the *"Primary Introduction",*

Please, always remember that if YOU are to take advantage of anything, take advantage of their *"senses" …*The *senses* that were indicated and discussed in Procedure 3. Now that YOU have **control** and have *created* and *established* a strong *"Relational Bond"* with your new acquaintance, they will actually help YOU along the way, by simply complying and enjoying themselves as they go!

Why, YOU might ask, is it that they are now in such compliance? Where earlier on in the *"Greet & Meet"* they seemed so *"stand offish"* and cold, not really interested in being helped, and stated that they were just looking, and now YOU have them in the palm of your hands, like butter on pancakes? So, to speak!

The answer my *"Friend"* and *"Confidant"* is as *simple* as this… *'process'* your new *awakening,* and like the *"Relational Bond"* that YOU *fashioned…* "EVERYONE" has come to their *"Senses"* to do *"What's Right"*, and that is to be *earnestly involved* and work *"together"* with the same outcome in mind!

It's always easier and more *congruent* to work together when *"Integral Connections"* have been established. Which is an easy transition when the correct questions are initiated and acted on by observing what it is that makes them...

"Hot to Trot" over, a "Hot" topic, or even a "Hot" item (*something that makes them eager to engage with or participate in*)! Hence the term *"Hot Buttons"*.

"Hot Buttons"

In a nut shell... *"Hot Buttons"* are *"Relational Connectors"* that are *congruent* to what it is that *entices* the Guest/Prospect/Consumer and *enhances* their...

"Ownership Decision Awareness"!

All *Guests/Prospects/Consumers* have put themselves in the position to be **"SOLD"** something (*Earned/Closed*) and then become *"A Customer"* the first moment that they initiated a *"Metamorphosis"* scenario, or a *"transition state of affairs"*. Let's expand on the term *"metamorphosis"* ... a 'metamorphosis' is a **change** or **shift**, 'relating' to a *"Paradigm Shift"*... ('*a pattern or a standard state of mind that is shifted from one place to another or one thing to another'*).

When a person's thoughts or ideas are *intervened* with *"to their benefit"*, the *process* of *"Metamorphosis"* falls into the *"Category of Simplicity"*. Because remember... a *"customer wants what they want when, "they want it!"*, and I am fully *confident* to believe of course, that YOU know that YOU *possess* the ***"want/desire"*** to create that ***"want"*** and ***"transition"*** (*"metamorphosis"*) with-in your ***"Prime Opportunity"*** …from a ***"Prospect"*** to an ***"Owner/Customer"***!

"YOU <u>CAN</u> DO IT!!!", and "I KNOW IT"!!! And believe me, more than YOU may actually realize it yourself!! Sometimes you just have to take baby-steps to get from point A to point B and stay in touch with your "true" self!

Back to ***"Hot Buttons*** as YOU *orchestrate* and ***"<u>lead</u>"*** your way to the ***"Close"***!

(***"<u>A</u>lways <u>B</u>e <u>C</u>losing"-<u>ABC</u>***)!

YOU are <u>NOT</u> a *"babysitter"*, nor is your *Guest/Prospect/Consumer* an infant, and they definitely do not want to be treated as such, nor in a *condescending* demeanor! Although they may have more *judgments* than *accurate information*. These are merely immature *"thought patterns"* about what it is that they are inquiring about. Which to a certain extent is a form of infancy. I would term this as *"Ownership Infancy"* …

"The early life of beginning to accept ownership".

While YOU are in the *"inquisition role"*, ensure that you are always fully aware of the *Guest's/Prospect's/Consumer's* ***"Hot Buttons",*** and that your *delivery* is in a manner that ***"<u>ties down</u>"*** your ***"Opportunity"*** with '*confident commitments'*. This also includes your *"physical demeanor",* proper *annunciation, inflection,* and the *verbiage* that YOU <u>choose</u> to use! YOU have to be *articulate, aware, sincere, focused,* and <u>YOU</u> have to be…**"Self-Motivated"** for ***"Right Reason"!***

To determine the ***"Right Reason",*** YOU need to be *astute* enough to not only understand what it is that *intrigues* your soon to be ***"Buyer/Owner,*** but also *perceptive* enough to *observe* the ***"comprehension level"*** of that soon to be *"Owner",* and what it is that they can, and will <u>*accept*</u> as a

benefit to, and for them. There's a ***"Hot Buttons"***, and it's that button (*indicator*) that will establish ***"Relational Connections"*** and create a ***"Relational Bond"***! Push the ***"Right"*** buttons and YOU will "push" your Opportunity/Consumer toward being a ***"Proud Owner"***, without being pushy! Go figure!

"Customer Involvement"

Now it's time to *articulate* on ***"Customer Involvement"*** ...This is a very a ***crucial element/ingredient*** not only in the process of ***"What's Right"***, but for any selling process. For the ***"FACT"*** that in order to get ***"The Order"***, YOU cannot complete this task without the Guest's/Prospect's/Consumer's... ***tangible*** and ***verbal involvement***!

To be "***involved***" is to be '*engaged*', and to be engaged is to be '*connected*'. '***Connected***'; (*v.*) '*to link up*', or (*v.*) '*relate to*' to have an "***interest in***", or most importantly, to have ***"Participation In"***! By having a <u>clear</u> "*point of understanding*" of the *importance* of getting the Guest/Prospect/Consumer "***involved***", not only during your **Presentation/Demonstration**, but just as *relevant* to sign any papers to finalize the process! Don't forget that the *relevance* here is, it all begins "***From Hello***"!

"Continued Involvement"

It really is a *"simple process"* to get a Guest/Prospect/Consumer involved. All one has to do is <u>make it fun</u> and <u>enjoyable</u>! Again, without being pushy! Have your *Prospect/Consumer* be pushy by having them pushing buttons, literally. By having your *Prospect/Consumer* do some things for themselves, especially in this *"Self-Service Age"* that we all seem to *enjoy,* or maybe got caught-up into. When a *"Consumer"* is given the *liberty* to actually be involved by touching and operating things themselves, especially something that they are, or maybe considering spending money on (*invest; getting something in return; R.O.I.*), and **"*own*"**. This gives your *Guest/Prospect/Consumer* a feeling or sense of **"*value*"**, and not considered *insignificant, ignorant* or *incapable*. The soon to be a **"Satisfied Customer"** will move themselves into their own *"comfort zone"*, giving them the impression that it is they that are the ones in *control*, and not being led, or worse, *"led-on"*!

It becomes harder for an **"*involved individual*"** to part with whatever it is that *captivated* their *attention* and or *resolved concerns*. This creates a **"Personal Connection"** of emotion to whatever, or even whomever it is that is being presented to them. Treat your *Opportunity* as a *participant,* by having them '*touch*', '*move*', or '*adjust*' things for themselves!

This will create a *"Personal Relational Bond"* directly with the product that YOU are presenting to the *Prospect/Consumer"*, by simply having them directly and **physically involved**. This not only creates a *"Tangible Experience"*, but also an experience that they will *appreciate* as well. Having your *Guest/prospect/Consumer* **"physically involved"** will actually get them **"emotionally involved"** to the point that they will not feel like *"shoppers"*, but as soon to be **"Proud Owners"**!

This part of the **"What's Right"** *process/technique* is where the *Prospect/Consumer* will actually have that *euphoric* feeling of **"Emotional Ownership"** throughout the entire *"Presentation & Demonstration"*, as long as YOU have assessed *accurately*, and that YOU are guiding *effectively*! It is throughout this *Procedure* where YOU target your *"Tie-Down Questions and Statements"* like a "chess move", progressing toward "Checkmate!!! When it comes time to *"Present and*

Demonstrate", to be in *"full control"* of the *"guidance process"*, YOU, actually have to be the one in the *"Driver's Seat"* when it's time for a *"Ride n' Drive"* ... Which reminds me of another story of interest...

As we segue into *"The Demonstration"*, most have it backwards once again. Let me explain...

"The Demonstration"

...All (3) of the auto dealerships of which I had the privilege to work with, as well as any dealership that I have ever visited, used the same process of having the *Consumer* drive off the premises (lot), instead of the "Sales Rep". Now I understand that this process is designed to get or have the *Prospect/Consumer* physically involved, and yes, they are most certainly physically involved as they are driving off the lot, but stop and ask yourself, and see if you're not as confused as I am...Who is actually in control of the situation here, is it YOU, or is it they? Think about it...who's in the driver's seat, when it is they that are *"driving"* off the lot/premises? Hello!

The *"Demonstration Drive"* is devised to **demonstrate** a product in detail with full understanding of the one being demonstrated to. This is where the confusion sets in. How can one demonstrate in detail, when YOU are not in the *"driver's seat"*. I also understand that a *"prospective buyer"* will indicate that they want to drive the product and may show signs of offense if not given the first opportunity to do so. They will even state things like..." *Don't you trust me?* or..."*don't I get to drive?"*

Here's what YOU say..."*Well most certainly Mr. Customer* (use their name), *I was hoping that I might have the liberty of chauffeuring you around, so you can experience what your family or guests will be experiencing when you*

Procedure 6 — Presentation & Demonstration

chauffeur them around, not to mention that by me driving off the lot, you will also be given an opportunity to experience the feel of the ride and comfort that this "xyz vehicle" truly has to offer, without any traffic distractions and such, also the experience of contentment knowing that your passengers or riders are as safe, and as comfortable as you are...Then I'll get to kick-back as you chauffeur me around, how does that sound Mr. Customer?... I have gotten a "Yes" every time.

Now, think about this one...If YOU let your *prospective buyer* drive off the lot, are YOU confident that your *Guest/Prospect/Consumer* knows where he or she is going, and will this drive show-off what the product truly has to offer? Not to mention, will they honestly get everything out of the experience without any negative activities or distractions that may take place in the driving world that we drive in? Drive them to a close and quiet area where you can make a safe transition, and butterfly the vehicle...this is where YOU, in a *Demonstrating* fashion, open all doors, hood and trunk, **Presenting** and **Demonstrating** along the way. This is known as *"a-walk-around"*, which can be done in less than five minutes!

Many "Sales Reps" have a tendency of taking the easy way out or are just merely unaware of the importance of maintaining **"smooth control"**, being just as important as a **"smooth landing"**!

By maintaining control of the situation and allowing your soon to be **"*owner*"** an opportunity to calmly enjoy and *investigate* whatever it is that **entices** him/her to this particular item or scenario. This will also put them in a *state/mood* of not feeling pressured or dictated to, and a state that it is they that are directing themselves, although it is YOU that is actually doing the directing, by allowing your *Prospective Buyer* to snoop at their **"*OWN*"** leisure, by lifting, moving things, pushing buttons or merely asking questions or making *"Personal Adjustments"* on the things that *interest* them to

"Their Satisfaction"! At the same time, this will give YOU another opportunity to notice those _"Hot Buttons"_ that trip their trigger. Another important factor to the _"test-drive"_, is to designate a specific route that not only fits the product that is being demonstrated, but also shows off the product to the utmost degree. It does not only have to be the enjoyment of the product, it can also be a scenic route that puts your _Guest/Prospect/Consumer_ in a calm and relaxed state-of-mind, assisting in the...

"Decision making/ownership process"!

By the time it is their turn to take over at the helm, they will be more at ease, and more familiarized with whatever it is that they are interested in, or concerned about., as well as a more comfortable feeling of their surroundings (_geographically, you and the product_). This practice will also give YOU the same opportunity to observe and get more familiarized with your _Guests/Opportunity_ and be in the moment of what it is that they are experiencing, except YOU already know the product and all that it has to offer, but do YOU know your soon to be **_Owner_** just as well. This is your _"Grand Opportunity"_ to study him/her on exactly what it is that entices them to an _"emotional state"_, and the best likelihood to accept everything that YOU are _presenting_ and _guiding_ them toward... _"Ownership"!_

As YOU _manage_ and _maintain_ your control (_"guidance-control"_) of this very important situation, ensuring that your _Guest/Prospect/Consumer_ is **_"completely assured"_** that YOU have his/her best interest at _"HEART"_ and it is to **_their benefit_**!

When this is the case, your _Guest/Prospect/Consumer_ will follow YOU to the moon and back, with a full _understanding_, _trust_, and a _desire_ to **_buy_** and **_own,_** from YOU!

Procedure 6   Presentation & Demonstration

Let's not forget, it is YOU that is the *"professional"*, with all the *pertinent* **product knowledge** and *"Proper Directing"* skills! By the time YOU arrive back to the dealership, YOU should have fired-off all your *"Trial/Trail Closes"*, and be fully re-loaded with all the ammunition needed to *"**consummate the deal**"*, and just as critical, your soon to be a *"**proud owner**,* should be as **connected** as YOU in regards to **making a "DEAL" happen**! If not, it's all on YOU to make an *evident* difference between YOU and your *"**competition**"*, or *"**the other guy**"*, so your *"opportunity"* doesn't become that *distant buyer* elsewhere. Confirming the fact that there is no such thing as a *"Be-Back"*!

You know you're in trouble, when Your *"Guest/Opportunity"*, says…" *Boy howdy Mr./Ms. Salesperson, I sure appreciate all the time and effort you spent with me/us, as well as all the information that you provided! We'll "Be-Back", do you have a card?*

Time to be either proud and over confident, yet humble and polite and present your card in the hopes that this very nice person in front of you is going to have the same opinion of YOU, as YOU have in yourself, and *"Be-Back"*, or, with the same demeanor, you politely excuse yourself to go get one of your cards, and **T.O.** (*Turn-Over the Company's Opportunity to someone else, so this opportunity is Taken-Over for a 2nd. Opportunity*)!

Do not take offense of this procedure, nor at yourself if you choose to **T.O.** For at this particular time of events, once that *Guest/Opportunity* leaves, YOU and **The Company** that depends on You, have ***absolutely nothing***! Even if You were fortunate enough to acquire contact info such as an e-mail address and or phone number. Good job for at least taking the extra effort to achieve this part of your required responsibility to acquire this info, but realistically speaking, it was not a "Great Job"! YOU and the Company still have nothing that can be taken to the bank, so to speak, nor a connected link.

Just a hope and a dream! Don't get me wrong, there's nothing wrong with hopes and dreams, in fact, when I was a local on-air radio personality, I would always close my show with... " *Always hang on to your hopes and dreams, because they can come true!"* Which was to be interpreted as in life's whole scheme of things. Not a One-Time shot, or at least in this type of scenario!

I am confident to believe that your esteemed self is sitting there thinking as YOU read along, that if one has contact info, an *"opportunity"* can be regenerated. Well, in the day before all the new technology was at a *Consumer's* finger tips, this most certainly may have been the case. Now add competition to these technologies, (**Competitive Internet Sales**), one is then linked to conveniences that will benefit them by possibly making things easier and convenient for them to make a decision. (*price shopping*). This is why, when YOU have been given, possibly of a *"Blessed Opportunity"* to have a *Guest/Prospect/Consumer* live and in person in front of YOU, it is very *imperative* to be one-step ahead of the game (***The Competition***), by knowing what's really going on down the street! This entails **_effort_** and **_diligence_** and that is acquiring a...

"Panoramic Commitment of Product Knowledge"!

Let's take *"product knowledge"* to a whole new dimension of *"Product Awareness"* where most *"Presenters and Demonstrators"* miss the mark by not investing the **_time_** and **_effort_** to **acquire** the same knowledge and understanding of the competition's product, and in some cases, even to the extremities of more than the competition's presenters themselves!

Procedure 6   Presentation & Demonstration

This next step is very crucial to your success in getting the *Guest/Consumers* to accept ownership of the product and or service that YOU are representing and presenting to them, ensuring that they have a complete "*acceptance of understanding*" of whatever it is that you are representing is a better value to them! Let's not forget that this *Guest/Prospect/Consumer* is a total stranger and You're attempting to convince this total stranger to accept ownership from YOU, a total stranger.

Here's a brief story and example that pertains to having all of the extensive product knowledge that is required to **get the job done and make things "*Happen*"**, as well as the *confidence* in whatever it is that YOU are so dedicated to **Present, Demonstrate** and **Sell**! This means, not having the *Prospect/Consumer*" leave, and go to the competition, but actually having the soon to be ***buyer/owner*** telling YOU...

... *"That there is no need to go to the competition!"*

Here I was waiting for an opportunity to drive up, being that I was up a raring to go to sell a car. A middle-aged couple drive up in a 4- or 5-year-old car, well let's just say, not a Toyota, which I was selling at the time. Anyways, as they pull up and park, I do my normal observations of these soon to be buyers/owners as they exit their vehicle. They were dressed well and appeared to have an appearance of inquisition in their facial expressions, first looking around, then gazing in my direction. I took this as a positive gesture of opportunity, therefore I gradually started to approach them while saying hello and welcoming them to the dealership of which I was representing and thanking them for being there. All the while getting closer to do a personal/professional meeting with an introduction, a handshake and name exchange. Once finding out the reasoning for this visit and their interest, I lead them to the New Camry area and began asking pertinent questions that pertained to their interests, narrowing it down to a specific unit (car). After completing a ride and drive (*demonstration*), *and upon returning to the dealership, asking relevant "trail-close" questions* (*tie-downs*) ...

This story will resume in the next Procedure "**_Making it Happen_**" ...The "Close"!

What's Right
Doing it For "The Opportunity"
Not to, "The Opportunity"

Procedure 7
"Making it Happen"
For
Customer
"The Close"

Procedure 7 — Making it Happen

That's *"Right"* ... *"Time to make it Happen", for "The Opportunity"* (*The Consumer*)!

By applying all that has been presented to YOU thus far in the previous steps of this *"Procedural Process"* of *"Betterment"*!" *Making It Happen"* should be a no brainer! Providing that YOU have guided effectively your soon to be **OWNER** at this point along the **Trail** to **Ownership** Notice that I used the term *"Trail"* and not *"Trial"* to" close"? Of which I term as *"Trail-Close"*!

Allow me to define why *"Trail-Close"* and NOT *"Trial Close"* ...First, let's expand on the word/term *'Trail'* as it pertains to normal uses in terminology and understanding, e.g. *"Trail to Fame and Fortune"*, "Trail *of Bread*crumbs" and of course *"Happy Trails to you"*! **Synonyms:** (*n.*) *'track', 'tail', 'path', 'route', 'roadway',* (*v.*) *'follow', 'pursue', 'tail',* etc.

By focusing on the above terms that I have chosen and the synonyms that were selected, are to exemplify a very relevant connection of what it is that YOU are doing (***Putting into action***), with and for whom YOU have invested all your time and energy with, procedurally speaking (*The Betterment Process in YOU that has been instructed thus far*)! The word "Trail' and the aspects of which are indicated and how they play an important role of in-common factors in which YOU are doing (*materializing*) with and for your *Guest/Opportunity*, and that is leading them along a **"Buying Journey"** and or ***"Complete Satisfaction"***, for the time of which they have also invested following YOU around! That is if YOU have been in complete control of the responsibility and situation at hand! Once again, ***"procedurally"*** speaking!

Think about this one... A leader without any followers is merely going for a walk!

By utilizing a *"paradigm shift"* in your **"train of thought/thought process"**, this most certainly makes a lot of sense!

Now let's do the same and expand on the word/term **'Trial'**, as it is normally associated with in today's society, merely to validate my point! e.g.; *"Trial and Error"*, *"Trial and Tribulation"*, *"On Trial"*, *"Trial Test"*, etc. **Synonyms**: (*n.*) *'ordeal'*, *'aggravation'*, *'suffering'*, *'annoyance'*, *'frustration'*, *'inconvenience'*, *'irk'*, *'peeve'*, *'pest'*, *'worry'*, *'difficulty'* …The list of **derogatory** "*word associations*" goes on and on, therefore I'll just stop there and state, etc.; For I'm sure YOU get my point!

The common factors that these words *connote*, are definitely in the derogatory status and are *connotation* that one really does not want to be associated with, on either side of the fence, so to speak!

Naturally it is obvious which one makes more sense than the other regarding the connotations, and the *relevance* of what it is that YOU do and what YOU are doing! Now, if You had to "choose" which **course** to take, which course would that be? The "Choice" is always up to YOU!

When You choose the verbiage and train of thought (*thought process*) "Trail-Close" instead of "Trial-Close" You have a *"successful understanding"* that is *congruent* to the "Betterment Process" of doing… *"What's Right"* in YOU, for the Opportunity!

Here's another contradiction in terms which make no sense at all when pertaining to acquiring (*earning*) a **"Customer"**, and that is the term **"Close"**, Time to **"Close"** the deal; Are they **"Closeable"**? How many deals did you **"Close"**? To **"close"**, is to; (*v.*) *'shut'*, *'finish off'*, *'terminate'*, *'wrap-up'*, *'conclude'*, *'come to an end'*, *'block'*, *'plug'*, *'obstruct'*, etc.; (*n.*) *'end'*, *'conclusion'*, *'completion'*, etc.

You most certainly don't want things to *"come to end"*! (More on how this will never happen in Procedure 8 *"Branding the Brain and the 7 R's"*)

Being that the ***"Betterment Process"*** of doing ***"What's Right"*** is *"structured"* to be fair and just, as well as *honest* in and to all that applies, including all these in-common factors (*words*)! It would only be fair to define a '*positive connotation*' of the word and or term '*close*', and that is when you close or shut something, you create a **seal** or **bond**, if you will...a *"Sealed Promise"*, a *"Bond of Trust"*, and this is exactly what needs to take place when associating (*dealing/relating*) with *"Consumers/Customers"*!

"Are they Closeable?" Absolutely not. The question is, Are they *"OPENABLE"*? ...Open to your directions and or suggestions for their business to be **"EARNED"**?

And do YOU have enough *faith* in YOU that they will allow themselves to move forward along the *"Trail"* of which YOU have been *guiding/leading* them in along the *"path"* to a buying decision? I will discuss "faith" and its importance to ***"The Close"*** in just a moment.

Think about this one...The term, *"The Close"*, or *"to be Closed"*, to a *"Consumer"*, and let's not forget, we are all *"Consumers"* at one time or another, and even YOU and I don't like to be "Closed". There's an old adage that states... "*salespeople are the easiest to be sold*". Why is this? Salespeople have a good understanding and comprehension level of the "*cat and mouse*" routine that takes place, and that most salespeople are notorious for (*guilty of*)! Therefore, negating the process, and simply saying yes!

Please take note that I am referring to "salespeople", not 'clerks', and no offense to be implied if You are in a clerk position/profession. Although if this be the case, then I have a note of suggestion for You as well! And that is, You have the same '*capabilities*' and '*opportunities*' as any sales person, just a different routine and or process category. Yet usually the same **"structure"**! That is relating to "*Customers/People*" in a '*professional*' and '*caring*' manner to their... **"Complete Satisfaction."**

The fact exists; "*The Soon to be Customer*" must be totally '*intertwined*' in order to make a decision to accept ownership of whatever it is that is being presented and or suggested to them. That is whether they are earnestly interested in, or merely reaching out to inquire information about the product and or service that is being offered. This is where YOU come into the picture, whether it be in obligation, or being just as earnest as they and wanting the same results, and that is '**earned**' and or '**maintained**' business with... **"Complete Satisfaction"**!

When it involves spending money, people would rather be in the category of being "*earned*", rather than being sold to! When put in this perspective, it should be fully understood and accepted that "*Customers'/People*" have that '**earned right**', for it is they that worked hard and earned a dollar to be spent on something of their interest. When this takes place, and someone gives You the '*opportunity*' to get them to spend their hard-earned money with You, don't blow it! You are the one to get the task at hand accomplished, providing that You have a complete understanding that a future "*Customer*" has to be **"Open to You"**, and the direction that You are leading them in, and that is them leaving as "*Happy Campers*" with '*Ownership/Satisfaction*' in their existence!

Now the importance of Faith when it comes to "closing the deal'. First of all, to be of no offence to One's intellect on the subject of "Faith" for knowing what it means is a no brainer to most, but not always adhered to at the Right moment! Here's the kicker...Not all actually "have the faith" when it comes to earning one's business in the now! To make my point let's break the word "faith" down in another synonym thesaurus research to find actual depth of its meaning; **'faith'** (*n.*) *'confidence'*, *'assurance'*, *'trust'*, *'reliance'*, *'conviction'*, *'belief'*, *'devotion'*, *'commitment'*, *'dedication'*, *'loyalty'*, etc.

Here's is a few ways that **Merriam-Webster** defines "faith' outside the religious box... *'allegiance to duty or person', 'fidelity to one's promises', sincerity of one's intentions', 'complete trust.'*

To expand even further let's do a paradigm-shift to enhance a connection of faith that goes both ways (*YOU and your Opportunity*). The underlined words are the in-common factors between YOU and your soon to be a proud owner of satisfaction... (*task completed*)!

They had *confidence* and *assurance* that they would find a person that they could *trust* and have a *reliance* on to assist in finding what they are out and about for.

Once again up to YOU to put your new "*Customer*' in the **loyalty box** to maintain that **connection**! To assist in that process, you're going to appreciate Procedure #8 **'Branding the Brain and the 7 R's'**!

It makes '*lucrative sense*' when the task of earning one's business, starts with a paradigm-shift at the very beginning in earning one's business, and that entails ... **"Opening the Deal"** to a **"Consummated Agreement"**!

The '*consummation process*' becomes a whole lot more satisfying to all involved, knowing that one is **'open'** to ideas and or suggestions! Being led, rather than being pushed and closed! Definitely a much better '*opportunity for success* for all involved!

Approach your new **"Opportunity"** from the very beginning with the attitude of **"opening"** or beginning a **"New Relationship"**, ensuring that your **"Guest/Opportunity"** is _open_ to all your directions, and suggestions! Now here is another important factor...I really hate so to say it, *"Closing the Deal"*. When YOU are making suggestions, ensure that they are implied as being **_honest_** and **_truly concerned_** suggestions, and not *"Condescending Direction"*. This will enhance the opportunity to completely **_"Open the Deal"_** to a '*consummated success*es, for Yourself, the Company, and again, most importantly... **"The Customer!"**

This next step is very crucial to your success in getting the *"The Consumer"* to accept ownership of the product and or service that you are representing, and that is having complete knowledge of whatever it is that you're representing.

Bring attention to the most important factors that your *"radar sensors"* targeted in on, by physically getting the *Consumer* involved; For example...If it's a *"Safety"* issue.

There are many things that can be tangibly presented and compared to that will tie your opportunity down to a no brainer scenario that makes sense to their satisfaction in making a safe *'Ownership Decision'*!

As long as it's to **_"their benefit"_** ...*it will be to **_their_** Safety Satisfaction!!!*

Let's reiterate on the *"Tie-Down"* Close...

To tie the Customer down, you simply ask questions that are pertinent to their ideas of whatever it is that piques their interest and wording it in a way that gets them to say YES to, or to be in agreement with the question that is asked, possibly with some elaboration. When asking a question that implies, or requires a "*yes answer*", simply move your head in an up and down motion suggesting a positive response.

...For example, *"being that you are going to be using this car as transportation for your grandchildren, I'm confident to understand that you want a car that is proven to be built with high safety standards, is that correct?"* (head moving up and down in a yes motion). Being that safety in an important issue with them, you will get a "yes answer", which ties them down to that important safety issue, which will move them closer to a buying decision!

I finally came to an understanding shortly after September 11, 2001 (*9/11*), the importance of acquiring the ***proper*** and ***complete*** <u>product knowledge</u> while I was with a "Toyota" dealership selling against another #1 product, "Honda". I knew I was offering a superior product on many levels, but not all, dependant upon the *Customer's* opinions, needs, and or wants!

Being that the "Toyota Camry" was the #1 selling car in America at the time, as a presenter of this product, I had to justify to *"The Customers"* why the Camry was the #1 selling car in America, and why it would be to their best interest and advantage to own a Toyota instead of a Honda.

Here is a reiteration of the previous story that pertains to having all of the extensive product knowledge that is required to ***<u>get the job done and make things "Happen"</u>***, as well as the *confidence* in whatever it is that YOU are so dedicated to **Present, Demonstrate** and **<u>Sell/Close</u>**! This means, not having your ***<u>"Grand Opportunity"</u>*** leave, and go to the competition, and at the same time, having the *"Consumer/Opportunity"* telling YOU…

"There really is no need to go to the competition!"

On a cool September morning, in pulls a mid-size nicely kept 4-door sedan, out steps a casually dressed middle-aged couple. This is where, the ***"What's Right"*** awareness is of crucial <u>relevance</u> to begin the 'Engagement Process'!

*I very promptly with a cool, calm, yet enthusiastic attitude/demeanor, "**greet**" these nice-looking folks from a distance and welcome them to our establishment. I then shook hands with my Guests/Prospects and exchanged names. This action of engaging with these Guests/Opportunity ("People") started the **"Process"** to earn their business. With the proper questioning, and timing, I was able build a **"Bond of Trust**, which enabled me to determine what it was that was of most importance to their ownership decision.*

Determining that "safety" was one of the important factors to them, and having a compassionate concern for their safety, as well as their grandchildren's. I took advantage of the way a Camry was designed and manufactured, targeting in on the safety issues that were superior to its main competitor...

One of the most prominent factors of safety that Toyota incorporated into their build was steel tinsel strength in the fenders. This would become very evident, when actually getting down to the nitty gritty pertaining to safety. The nitty gritty is this...I had to have the product knowledge, not only in the product that I was representing and its advantages, but just as important, an acquired knowledge of the competitor's product that the Opportunity/ Consumer's interest and concerns were.

This is where you must have a '*true and complete*' understanding of the '*imperative concerns*' and what it is that intrigues your soon to be **Owner/Customer**, and the complete knowledge of what it is that you are presenting/selling to your *Opportunity/Consumer* in order for them to move forward to the *'ownership process'*. By simply getting the *Consumer* to have the same understanding, knowledge, and acceptance of the product and or service that you are representing and presenting to them. Now, you might think that this is part of the "*Demonstration and Presentation*" process, and yes, it is to a certain extent, for this reason...You must always be

Procedure 7 — Making it Happen

selling and demonstrating the product all the way through to the **"*Consummation Process*"** (*deal*), where the *Prospect/Consumer* accepts the idea/ideas of ***ownership*** of your product, ***tangibly*** and ***emotionally***!

This is where YOU must once again take the bull by the horn and pull out all the stops and put pants on your Hot-to-Trot (*ready to buy*) *Guest/Opportunity* and soon to be ***"Proud Owner"***!

Back to the Toyota/ Honda story…

*With my understanding of the two 'main objectives' that my soon to be owners had, which was safety and reliability. By adding a main competitor/contender (Honda). I had three main **objectives/objections** to overcome. I had to steer them first in the direction of the safety comparison elements of both products that were under investigation by this very well informed and enthusiastic want to be owner of one or the other product that they had so thoroughly researched, metaphorically speaking. For they had not been involved personally in a "Face to Face" environment where they had a chance to actually experience either product that was of their interest.*

This is where I led them into the showroom where we could be in a more conducive atmosphere where a more personal buying environment was present, as well as showroom condition vehicles that could be ogled over and demonstrated. I smoothly segued into the importance of my Guest's second objection, which was safety, go figure, reliability was their first objective. This being the reason that they allowed themselves to be there in front of originally a stranger, yet at this point and time of the process I had gained their trust and confidence in me, which made them putty in my hands, therefore I could suggest and lead them to what I believed would be a primary factor in their buying decision, and that was the tinsel strength in the front fenders. I first discussed the subject matter, and then I reached down and grabbed the fender firmly and attempted to move it back and forth with no avail. I then had Mr. Prospect/Consumer repeating what I just exemplified to him. Needless to say, he was highly impressed.

Now, here's the kicker...To be fair and to solidify my point of safety superiority over my competitor, I took my soon to be owners outside to where the pre-owned vehicles were inventoried and led them to a 2-year-old pre-owned Honda of the same classification as the vehicle of which I had just presented, demonstrated, and had them drive earlier one in the process. Which was a new Camry. I then informed them to check out a comparison difference comparing the ride differences between the two products by having them drive a 2-year-old pre-owned Honda.

Hold on, we're trippin' now, "pun intended". As we pull back into the dealership, Mr. Consumer now at the helm, I have him park next to a 2-year-old Camry and then had him drive it, indicating that both of the new products that were in question would get to be at least 2 years old and, in their possession, **/ownership** based on the info I acquired earlier in my 'fact finding' process/investigation. Therefore, giving them a tangible comparison where they could rationally evaluate the differences between the two products demonstrated. Giving them a "**multiple of choice**' decision of which vehicle felt safer and had the better and smoother ride qualities of a 2-year pre-owned car? They indicated that the pre-owned Camry had a ride very similar to the New Camry they had experienced earlier.

Now, get this, here they were contemplating a decision on the concept of a pre-owned (used) vehicle comparison, when they were actually in the market for a new one. The decision was actually based on the contemplation of either doing it this way (Toyota), or that way (Honda), not new or used.

Throughout my comparison presentation and demonstration of both products, I consistently mentioned when that they get to the "Honda" store, that this or that is what they should be asking about or checking out, for in some cases the competitor may not offer the information or may not know the actual differences. After the "***ride and drive***" comparisons and true "*fender popping*". I **'*tied*'** them down with a "***multiple choice***" question that would have them confirm verbally that my product had not only everything that they were interested in and concerned about. But, also having them verbalize their opinion, confirming the considerable advantages that were apparent over the competition.

It was at that time, I simply asked them,"*so when do you think you will be going to the "Honda" store?* Knowing where I was in the process. I was very confident that they would have no need to go to the Honda store. Not to my surprise, they answered...

"That there was really no reason to go to the Honda store (Competition)*!"*

All I had to do now, was work out the details to ***"Their Satisfaction"!***

At this point I escorted them into my office and ensured that I made them feel right at home. Being that they were the Company's and my *Guests*, I wanted, and needed them to continue to conform to my direction. Where at this time, I offered them beverages, which I would have in a small refrigerator adjacent to my desk. This implies that I am conscientious about my soon to be ***"Customer's"*** comfort and even well-being, on a minute scale. (*little things go a long way*)! As they are setting into a '*Comfort Zone*', this enables me an allotted time to retrieve all the pertinent information on the exact product/unit that these *People/Guests/Prospects/Consumers* will be proudly owning and driving home within the next hour or so.

Once I return, I sit across from my *Guest*, pull out my work/commitment sheet (*a.k.a. 4-Square*), then simply ask my soon to be owner... (*His or Her name*) "*once we work out all the details, how exactly would you like your new car titled?* They almost always say, "*in my name*". In return, this is where I cordially ask them for their driver's license, which has all their pertinent information that is required to complete the process of title and registration. This also keeps your now/new "*Customer*" involved by participating and also solidifies the **"*I just bought a car attitude*"**!

This next step in this portion of the "*consummation process*" (The Close) is crucial in the *verbiage/vocabulary* of which YOU choose. Earlier in the *Primary Introduction* I listed 101 "*words of relevance*", there are also words and phrases of "**irrelevance**" that should never be utilized... '*buy*', '*sell*', '*sign*', '*contract*', '*no*', '*can't*', '*I don't know*', '*not possible*' '*long wait*'.

Here are some replacement words that can be utilized instead of...**Buy;** '*own*', '*purchase*', '*invest*'. **Sell;** '*earn*', '*propose*', '*offer*'. **Sign;** '*approve*', '*ok*', '*authorize*'. The best replacement word or **Contract; '*agreement*'**.

From the very beginning of the "*Greet & Meet*" process with these *Guest/Prospects*, I "**assumed**" that they were in the market to buy, not in the market to look. Although they were in the looking stage. They were determined to look and see what Toyota had to offer, and later, find out what Honda had to offer. What they did not know is that it was I, that was going to actually make all the difference in their timing and buying decision!

When I mentioned that from the beginning of my "*Greet & Meet*" I "**assumed**" that they were "**buyers**"! This is a very important element to earning one's business, and it does start at the very beginning, not to be utilized only in the "**closing**" stage of the process, e.g. "**assumption close**".

Procedure 7 — Making it Happen

To **'assume'**; (v.) *'take for granted', 'presume', 'imagine', 'believe', 'affect', 'take upon yourself', 'take on', 'start or begin to have'*, etc.

By utilizing the "**Assumptive Thought Process**" YOU are assured in your *'state of mind'* that the **opportunity** that is in front of YOU is them to make a decision there and now, which gives YOU the upper hand from the very beginning by having an understanding that everyone there has the same **connection** (*in-common factors*), and that is **"Making it Happen'!** Now if that isn't an "**assumption**", I don't know what is!

As I mentioned earlier, *People/Prospects/Consumers* must "**emotionally feel ownership**" for the product that initiated their interest. When meeting *'face to face'*, they have allowed YOU to examine the situation and move them forward so that *'emotional connections'* can be established!

Here's another kicker…They aren't even aware that they have opened a Pandora's box of *'emotional connections'* and *'opportunity'* once they allowed YOU to shake their hand!

Let's define the term *'emotional connections'*; *'a psychological/psychosomatic pattern that takes place in the thought process that has been expanded on a personal level that establishes a state of euphoric bliss, creating a harmonious connection to whatever it is that satisfies one's "**emotional intentions**.'*

The story and scenario in which I depicted earlier indicates a prime example of "**emotional intentions**' and *'emotional connections*. These "Prospects" were there originally to compare products, and they knew what it was that was going to entice their buying decision. What they did not know was that what they were actually trying to accomplish (*main objection*) was to have a chance to experience both products. One thing they were not aware of is that both products would be available at the same place, being that what they were interested in was new, and they knew that Toyota only offered Toyota. Therefore, they would have to make two stops.

"***Emotionally***", they really didn't want to go through the process of looking and buying a car, let alone having to do it twice. They were simply looking for a '*resolution*'!

Since we reached a topic of **'*resolution*'**, let's see where that word takes us…'***Resolution***'; (*n.*) '*solution*', '*answer*', '*outcome*, '*end*', '*resolve*', *determination*', '*steadfastness*', '*perseverance*', etc.

Simply find the **"*Hot-Buttons*"** and expand on them by ensuring that YOU get on the same page as Your "*Guest/Prospect/Customer*", then **guide** them along the…

"*Path of Ownership*"
(Trail-Close to Partnership/Ownership/Relationship)!

There are many t*echniques* and *procedures* in closing the deal that are established and directed to get the **"*Prospect/Consumer*"** to <u>**say yes**</u>! And the task at hand is not a simple one to achieve without having some sort of technique and or process. The question is…is the '*technique*' and or '*process*' that YOU **choose** to **_EARN_** one's business, will it have **"Heart"**? Let's not forget that **"*People/Prospects/Consumers*"** have **"Heart"** …This is where the **emotion** comes from for them to make the decision to move forward to **buy** and **own** (*gut feeling*). It is YOU that is obligated to establish that "***Integral Connection***" that will allow YOU to move your opportunity forward in the same fashion, without *deception*, *trickery*, or a *ruse,* so that a… "*Relationship*" can be *established*, '*preserved*', and '*retained*'!

Note: Recommended read and practice…" *Secrets of Closing the Sale"!* Zig Ziglar

Other recommended reads…

- *"Low Profile Selling"* (*"Act like a Lamb, Sell like a Lion"*) Tom Hopkins

- *"Guide to Greatness in Sales"!* Tom Hopkins

- *"25 Sales Habits"* (*"…" of highly successful salespeople"*) Stephan Schiffman

- *"7 Habits of Highly Effective People"*; Stephen R. Covey

- *"Little Book of YES Attitude"*; Jeffrey Gitomer

- *"What Do Customer's Really Want?"*; John F. Lytle

- *"Discipline of Market Leaders*; Michael Treacy & Fred Wiersema

- *"The Service Payoff"*; Dr. Alan Zimmerman

- *"The Motivation Manifesto"*; Brendon Burchard

- *"The Sales Advantage"* (*"…" how to Get and Keep Customers"*) Dale Carnegie

- Any book by J. Douglas Edwards

What's Right
Doing it For "The Opportunity"
Not to, "The Opportunity"

Procedure 8
"Branding The Brain"
And "The 7 R's"

Responsibility-Respect-Rapport-Reputation
-Relationship-Retain-Refer

"Achieving Your Objectives Inevitably"!

This is where the *"Betterment Process"* of doing *"What's Right"* puts everything into a clear perspective and into overdrive, so that YOU can meet Your objectives head-on with great success. Now we know it starts with YOU, and Your attitude toward success! Here's an interesting fact for YOU, and that is without a physical being (***prospect/opportunity***) in front of YOU, YOU are basically unemployed, that is if you're on a commission basis pay-plan.

So, what do You do? Are You one to just sit there with a *hope* and a *prayer* that someone drives up or walks in and says that they are just there to merely buy something. Not that there is anything wrong with a lay-down and hopes and prayers, but like anything else, these "*Hopes and Prayers*" must be put in proper perspective, as well as proper priority, and let's not forget "realistic"!

I'm not going to elaborate at this time on what I believe and feel entirely about the topic of Hopes and Prayers, and what God has to do with it. That will be generated in my next book! *"Connection"* ... *"A Betterment Process to God"*

What we're all hoping for with a prayer is that someone comes in and buys something so that we can pay our way and cover our financial obligations (*objectives*), whatever they might be. When one has chosen a profession of associating with people, many other ***obligations/objectives*** arise in the scheme of things. With all these '*obligations/objectives*' that one now has on their plate, how in the world is one expected to "*accomplish them automatically/inventively*", and how is that possible? You might be asking!

The answer begins with the... *"The (7) Seven- R's", or, the "7- Are's"!* (not a proper word)

1. Are You Capable?
2. Are You Willing?
3. Are You Available?
4. Are You Passionate?
5. Are You Sincere?
6. Are You Motivated?
7. Are You Ready to Connect and Succeed?

If You answered YES to all the above, then YOU *"Are"* ready for the final equation for *"Branding the Brain"* to achieve *"**Customer Retention**"* and *"**Customer Referrals**"*, and it requires the 7-R's... *Responsibility-Respect-Rapport-Reputation-Relationship-Retain-Refer*

The *(7) Seven- R's* that are depicted in this not so final segment (*procedure*) are not only required and **relevant** to the *"Betterment Process"* of doing *"What's Right"*, but just as important if not more so in order to **brand the brain** properly with great success!

If you're really '*sincere*' about doing *"What's Right"* in all that YOU do, then I am very confident that YOU are curious enough at this particular time in this tutorial read (*"Betterment Process"*), to ask "what exactly is **Branding the Brain** and it's '*process*'?"

And let's not forget it takes *heart*! Now, allow me to ask YOU a question..."is your heart really in it? If it is, **"YOU'RE IN IT TO WIN IT"**!!!

First let's begin with *"Branding the Brain"* ...What it is and how do YOU do it?

To *"Brand the Brain"* requires **diligence, passion, motivation, and consistency!**

To brand the brain or as it is actually termed, ***"Branding the Brain"*** is a Marketing and Advertising term and a very consistent practice which requires one more ingredient, and that is money. The money that is *spent/invested* is of great magnitude. So much so that the 2023 Super Bowl commercial cost for a mere 30 second spot (commercial) ranged between $6 million and $7million. If that is not a great magnitude of dollars being spent, then I don't know what is!

Now, to validate that ***"Branding the Brain"*** works, here the proof…what company do YOU think of first when pizza comes to mind? Let's try a few others…Tacos? Beer? Chicken? Cola? Burgers?

By a vast majority these are the answers that most would readily recall…

Pizza; *"Pizza Hut"*, Tacos; *"Taco Bell"*, Beer; *"Budweiser"*, Chicken; *"KFC"* (*Kentucky Fried Chicken*), Cola; *"Coke"*, Burgers; *"Mc Donald's"*.

Well, what name *"**Brands**"* (*Companies*) came to your mind or recalled without even having to think that hard about it? All the name brands that were chosen by a vast majority are all household names and are International, validating as proof that the ***Branding the Brain*** process works with big payoffs in order for the dollars being spent, turning into investment dollars. Be assured that these Companies are getting a good Return on their Invested *Marketing* dollars (R.O.I.). Being Internationally renowned, these Companies have proven that it pays to "Market" and "Advertise" their product.

Here are some numbers to give YOU a better comprehension of the invested dollar that was spent for a 30 second commercial in Super Bowl LVII (57) 2023. Based on Nielson Ratings, over 50 million homes were tuned in equating to over 113 million viewers, which is almost a third of the population of which was targeted. With that many viewers also be assured that many brains were *'Brand Strengthened'*, being that viewers have not only experienced these products, but have also been bombarded with *'Brand Imaging'* on a <u>consistent</u> basis! I am not trying to indicate profit margins and such, just merely making a point on *'Brand Exposure'* and to give YOU a greater understanding of the strength of what *"Branding the Brain"* actually has to offer as an investment term.

Here's another prime example of how *"Branding the Brain"* works and succeeds on a local level.'

As I mentioned earlier a Company named "United Bedrooms" and the success with 7 locations (*showrooms*) in the Phoenix Metropolitan area. When I first came aboard, there was only 1 location, and I was the first sales representative. This first location was merely a humble 2,500 sq. foot unit in a small strip center, which included warehousing of the humble inventory. Don't forget we ended up with 7 locations in 5 years, 6 of which were elaborate showrooms measuring 7,500 to 10,000 sq. ft. with a separate warehouse and corporate office location.

This was all accomplished by *"Branding the Brain"* with saturated and consistent marketing campaigns, utilizing 75% radio advertising on 7 to 9 major radio stations on a consistent routine. The radio stations that were selected were the ones with peak ratings. The other 25% was divided between TV and print advertising. On each "Grand Opening" it was always a big hoopla with live-remote broadcasts, clowns, in the sky flood lights, even a rented sharecropper's aircraft (*2 person airplane*) with a banner on the tail end reading…**UNITED BEDROOMS!!!** By this time, I was also a big success where I had reached the plateau of Regional Sale Manager with an average of 50 sales reps and 14 Managers under my supervision and direction.

All this takes place in a short period of a little over 5 years by simply having a **_vision_** and **_goal_** with a **_plan_** with tons of **_motivation_**! The plan was to open a showroom once a year or less, and to do that money was needed on a consistent basis and in volume. It was evident to the owner that the best place to get money was from either robbing a bank or from **Consumers** (people). So, the owner decided to take advantage of the "thing" at the time, and that was waterbeds, which required people to be successful by turning them into **Consumers**. Hence the reason to utilize the *"Brand the Brain"* strategy! *"Branding the Brain"* worked so well that the Phoenix Metropolitan area became the waterbed capital of the world with a total of 5 competitors. A total of 26 locations where a Consumer could buy a waterbed.

As quoted by renown Chinese Philosopher Lao Tzo...
"The key to growth is the introduction of higher dimensions of consciousness into our awareness."

We have covered the process of *"Branding the Brain"* on a grand scale and a medium scale, so one might ask..." how do we *"Brand the Brain"* on a smaller scale when it's *"face to face"* or *"one on one"*?

The answer is rather simple; once again, providing you're **_truly in it to win it_**! And YOU can do it with a very small investment dollar or none at all. It depends on your '*ability strength*' to think and '*motivate*' outside the normal box that has been instilled in most Sales Associate/Representatives, and that is being '*lackadaisical'*!

Being that the word '*lackadaisical*' is not a commonly used word and is the <u>opposite</u> of all that has been presented to YOU thus far and forever more! Allow me to expand on it... '*lackadaisical*'; (adj.) '*lax*', '*apathetic*', '*lazy*', '*relaxed*', '*laid-back*', '*half-hearted*', etc.

Time for a Paradigm-Shift if YOU fall or have ever fallen into this category!

Time for the *7 R'S*, the answer; Hot to **"*Brand the Brain*"**, and it does not require a branding iron nor heat. Although it does require making a **mark**!!!

The 7 R's have been created to do just that…" make a mark" …and YOU are that "MARK"!

All the Companies of which I have previously mentioned, advertise not just their product to create a **"*Brand*"**, but also their "name" with a logo to accentuate their image, which heightens the *"Branding Process"* to make that **"mark"** on the brain. And they do it on a consistent basis. Which must take place in order for the *"Brand"* to stick! When a Consumer is in the market for, or a craving for, this is where that **"*mark*"** pays off!

The point…**PROMOTE** and **ADVERTISE YOURSELF!!!**

The word *"Mark"* may be in the derogatory term category, although one does need to make an impression that sticks like a "*mark*" … *"The Mark of Greatness"!*

It starts with the first '*R*'; ***Responsibility…***The most fundamental and important part of anything YOU do, is being **"*Responsible*"** for yourself and the action that YOU choose to take as well as being '*conscientious*' enough to move forward with a positive mental attitude (PMA), or should I say, a *"winning attitude"*!

I'm confident to believe that we all have an astute understanding of what it is to be *"responsible"*, but as a mental strength enhancer on the subject, lets expand on the thought process of being *"responsible"* ... here are a few synonyms that are, and should be related to reach any level of success...

(*adj.*) *'accountable'*, *'dependable'*, *'conscientious'*, *'trustworthy'*, *'reliable'*, *'mature'*, *'in charge'*, etc.

Now, with an enhanced mental picture of what it requires to take on a *responsibility,* or *responsibilities*, YOU have begun the ***"Branding the Brain Process"***. YOU have to begin the **process** of *"Branding the Brain"* with yourself, which moves us to the 2nd. *'R'*; *Respect*...not just for Your *Guest/Prospect/Opportunity*, but all involved, and that includes, YOU! You must have enough *'respect'* in yourself knowing that all that YOU do is on Your shoulders, and the choices YOU make can either hinder or enhance YOU, and the <u>opportunities</u> that may cross your path.

What is *'Respect'*? Let's define it in relational terms, e.g. (*n.*) *'esteem'*, *'reverence'*, *'regard'*; (*v.*) *'value'*, *'appreciate'*, *'regard'*, *'recognize'*, *'acknowledge'*, *'accept'*, *'follow'*, etc.

Now, select the relational words that YOU feel are the most relevant regarding a *Guest/Prospect/Opportunity*! Then maintain a focus on your chosen words and use that thought process to generate the same thought process in your *Prospect/Opportunity in* regards of how they feel towards YOU. (*This is a form of mirroring in a subconscious state.*) Once *'Respect'* is gained, it opens the door to vast *"opportunities"*! Especially in the process of obtaining one's business!

"A little 'respect' goes a long way!" Boy are YOU in for a big surprise...keep reading!

Now we have *"Rapport"*, the 3rd. *'R'*; Rapport is probably the most essential ingredient in "<u>**Achieving Your Objectives Inevitably**</u>"*!* A good *'Rapport'* assists in building <u>trust</u> and *"Respect"*! We know that we have to institute a foundation of *'Respect'* from the very beginning, yet this cannot be established without a good **"*Rapport*!"**

Here is how "Rapport" relates to establishing ***"Customer Relationships"***, e.g. (*n.*) *'understanding', 'empathy', 'link', 'bond', 'attraction'*, etc.;

By incorporating the common words listed above, YOU can be assured that YOU will have established a good *'Rapport'* with your now *Owners/Customers*. Which will secure your communication as YOU move along to the ***"Retain and Referral"*** process.

One has to have the <u>understanding</u> that it is <u>empathetic</u> to take action that will produce an <u>attraction</u> that will **link** one with another in agreement, creating a ***"relational bond"*** that will **strengthen** the Salesperson's (YOU) <u>***"Reputation"!***</u>

If you noticed how *"Rapport"* segued into *"Reputation"*, that is the 4th. **'*R'*;** In order to acquire a good *'Reputation'*, one first has to have a good *"Rapport"* with people as well as self-respect, and an awareness of what people might think about them without being in a state of mind..." *what about me"?* I'm sure you've heard the term..." ***Your Reputation depends on it"***! Well, it does if you want to "Retain your <u>**Customers**</u> and have them ***"refer"*** other <u>**Consumers**</u> to YOU!

Here's a quick break down on One's ***"Reputation"*** ...'Reputation'; (*n.*) *'standing', 'status', <u>'name'</u>, <u>'character'</u>*, etc.

Notice, your <u>Name</u> and <u>Character</u> depends on it!

So, keep tabs on what it is that YOU are doing and <u>manage</u> your ***"Reputation"*** so that YOU can establish, build and ***"Retain"*** **Customer Relationships**!

Another segue... ***"Reputation"*** to ***"Relationships"*** ...

"Relationship" is a derivative of the word *'relation'*; which is the act of telling or recounting, also construed as an aspect or quality that connects two or more things as being or belonging together, or as being of the same kind; 1. (*n.*) *connection, association, parallel, bond, interconnection, relevance,* 2. (*n.*) *family member, relative,* or *next of kin.*

As YOU look and understand the synonyms that have *'relevance'* to the subject of connecting with a *'parallel association'*, YOU will also notice that it creates a personal if not a professional *'bond'* with your 'Opportunity', improving and strengthening your <u>opportunity</u> to earn your *Opportunity's* business, or in other words…treat your *opportunity/consumer* like a *family 'member/next of kin'*!

I sincerely hope you can honestly relate to the importance of relating in a conducive manner with your first shot at building a **<u>relationship</u>** with your *Opportunity/Consumer*! That's right…first shot, it all starts from hello, and you only get one shot at hello! First impressions are one the most important ingredients at building *relationships*, personal, and or professional! As Tom Cruise said in "Jerry Maguire" … *"you had me at hello"*!

Now it's time to add the **"<u>SHIP</u>"** to *'relation'*. The "ship" that is missing most certainly is not the "Titanic" (*The one that sank that is*).

Although the ship which I am referring to is somewhat "Titanic". That being *monumental* and of <u>significant</u> matter! The "ship" is very crucial in succeeding not only in **Relations** where YOU can then catapult the **Prospect/Opportunity** into Ownership, which is where <u>Partnerships</u> are spawned, and <u>Relationships</u> are consummated and **"Retained"**!

Time to move your **"Now Customer"** to the "**R & R Program"** (*Retain & Refer*) that YOU so diligently worked so hard for (*earned*)! Why YOU might ask; This where the **Betterment Process** of doing" What's *Right"* pays off!

First You must *"Retain"* your "now' *Customer* to get them out of the now category and put them in the "forever" more category. YOU evidently have earned that **'Right'**, being that YOU have come thus far with your *Opportunity!*

Think about this for a moment. I'm Going to turn the tide a bit to give YOU a stronger grip hold on the importance of retaining your *Customers* by comparing a Customer to the highest purchase that most people make, and that is a house. Which of course is an "Investment Purchase". Where in almost all cases make money.

What most people do once they are obligated to this grand purchase is they usually take *"CARE"* of it by maintaining it, or even adding on to it to increase its **value.** Also known as *"Betterment"!*

The point I'm making is this, and that is '**Value**'. By earning The Customer's worth (business), they now become of great value to the Company that YOU represent, as well as yourself! Time to continue taking care of your investment. That's right…INVESTMENT". Earlier I mentioned that things go full circle. Well, YOU spent (*invested*) all that time to get to a consummated deal (*earned business*). Are You going to merely spend that time (*time spent*) and be done with it, or are YOU going to continue investing that time for a R.O.I. (*Return On Investment*); and that is…

"***Return Business***" and "***Referrals***"!

Let's now go to the second highest purchase that most people make, and that is an automobile. Unlike a house purchase it's not an investment purchase, but a depreciating product, regardless of how one does or doesn't take care of it. This being the case people don't keep this purchase much more than 3 to 5 years on average. But let's not forget that a car is now considered a necessity, therefore a replacement will be in order. This is where YOU need to ensure that YOU did all the proper <u>maintenance</u> to ***"Retain"*** your investment (*Time and Customer*) for <u>Return Business</u> and **"Referrals"**!

This how YOU ***"Retain"*** your Customers...YOU have already initiated that <u>Branding Process</u> with yourself, and it worked because YOU won them over enough to earn their business. That's ***"Right"*** YOU did it! Now, don't drop the ball! Time for the big payoff for all the work and time that YOU have invested <u>thus far</u> and accomplished. Notice that I stated 'thus far' in the work (*efforts*) in which YOU have accomplished. This is because your efforts are not done. One is usually required to keep in touch with a Customer after the sale is made with a follow-up call. But many times, more so than not, Wrong Reason falls into play. A phone call is usually the communication format chosen for this follow-up contact, and unfortunately, it's usually a contact about a CSI survey...Wrong Reason!

The "survey" will take care of itself providing that YOU take care of your Customers before, during, and after the sale, with honest and earnest (*heartfelt*) content! And continue to do so with '***heartfelt ambition***' on a consistent basis!

Providing that YOU have done an accurate ***"Rapport"*** building process, I am confident to believe that some personal information was received...such as what they may like to do, or go, or maybe they spoke about their pet/pets or family members. Something that matters to them, enough to talk about with a stranger. These are the things that can be the reasoning for a follow-up contact call, or any other continued communication. For continued success the first follow-up contact should be about them and anything that has to do with them. Throughout your Relationship building process Stay in contact and or communication with your earned opportunity on a consistent basis without being a pain in the YOU know what! The variety of ways that can be selected to do so with today's technology is easier than ever. Which in turn, makes it a Yes-Brainer instead of a No-Brainer to *"Brand the Brain"* with images of YOU (*your name*)! Don't forget, YOU have already made an acceptable impression or an image of YOU in reality! So much so that YOU were allowed to earn their business by them!

Here are some other ways and reasons to keep in touch with your "Name" on it...

- Thank You Cards
- Birthday *Cards*
- Christmas Cards
- Anniversary Cards
- Special Event Invitation (*Business Connection*)

Just with these 5 reasons, one keeps their **"Name"** in front of *"The Customer"* (*"Brand Imaging"*)! With internet emails, phone messaging (text), etc.; this opens up a vast amount of contact/communication opportunities, where there is no reason/excuse not to be a skilled Brander!

It does not matter what it is that One is selling, or any other type of scenario that involves a **Consumer** or **Customer**, to *"retain"* them, "They" must first be **Completely Satisfied** with the Process that "They" experienced, and YOU must continue to *"Brand"* their brain with all this goodness (*Satisfaction*)!!!

Time for a referral...

By this time in the *"Betterment Process"* of doing *"What's Right"*, YOU have most certainly earned a **Referral!!!** That's *'Right'*, Referrals are earned!

The best time to connect for a *referral,* but not necessarily a time ask for one, is when it comes to your attention that

YOU received a completed survey indicating that your earned Customer is...

"100% Completely Satisfied"

Now is the time to contact your *"Completely Satisfied Customer"* once again and discuss the topic of a "Survey", being that YOU are now Completely Satisfied knowing that YOU succeeded in doing *"What's Right"* to earn that survey. The meaningful purpose for this next contact is to thank your *"Completely Satisfied Customers"* for taking care of YOU with a 100% Completely Satisfied Survey! Which by the way goes into the record books for an opportunity for more earned dollar opportunities!

The reasoning behind me stating that this contact is not necessarily the time to ask for a referral is that YOU do not want **"wrong reason"** to enter this grand *opportunity* to continue building and strengthening the Sales Professional/Customer Relationship bond. The reason for this contact, (*preferably by phone voice to voice*) is to show appreciation and again, strengthening that **BOND** (*the side that makes sense to 'close'*)

I am not stating that YOU couldn't ask for a referral at this time, it all depends on where YOU were in the communication and bonding process along your "trail" to earning their business. If YOU established a good rapport and created a strong bond personally, and professionally. You can ask for a *"Referral"* at any given time, or at least plant the seed. Although a more conducive time to plant a seed for a *"Referral"* or just be upfront and indicate in requisition, is once the business is earned!

Here's an example for a *"Referral Request"* ...

"If by chance Mr./Mrs. Customer (use their name) *you know anyone or come across anyone that I can be of any assistance, could you please let me know and will be happy to be of assistance. And if by chance I have what they want and they allow me to earn their business, you will get a Referral Fee!* In the car business this is called a "birddog", usually $100 or $200. Now ask them..." *how does that sound Mr./Mrs. Customer?"*

If your **"Customer"** comes back with a reply that is positive and agreeable, then respond with a direct requisition of whom it is that they know. Now YOU have the ball rolling, so to speak!

Here is a prime example of how and not how the **"Referral Process"** works toward the success of a Company, or its demise!

Refraining back to the "waterbed" story...

*The company that I mentioned "United Bedrooms"; with all the successes that were achieved, there was a serious glitch in their operation protocol and that was a process to **"Retain"** Customers. Which negated the Opportunity for **"Referrals"**. Which finally lead to their demise with the vast amount of competition that had sprung up. Mostly due to the popularity of waterbeds and the **Branding** that had taken place and achieved. Although me being in upper management, I not only didn't have full control of decisions being made, but there also was no Customer follow-up or retention program ever incorporated into operation protocol. For the reason that the owner had no true regard for the Customers that he had so rigorously baited and reeled in, and that Me and my TEAM had earned. One of the main competitors was a waterbed company that existed 6 years prior to United Bedrooms ever opening its first store, called "Oasis Waterbeds" with only 2 locations at the time of United Bedrooms materialization. By the time United Bedroom had achieved 7 locations, Oasis*

Waterbeds had grown to 5 locations. Another serious competitor was a company called "Sun Valley Water Beds", started by twin brother carpenters in their garage. At their beginning, they were merely 2 carpenters earning money on the side making waterbeds for local venders. Eventually opening their own store and ending up with 8 locations. I was offered a General Sales Manager's position with "Oasis Water Beds" and given the control to incorporate a "Customer Retention-Referral" program. Which is where I initiated the "7 R's"! Hence, this is where United Bedrooms failed... No Customer Retention Program! While with "Oasis Water Beds', we opened 4 more locations in a two-and-a-half-year period, totaling 9 locations. This was accomplished by having a Grand Opening Extravaganzas, and also having the sales staff contact every earned Customer in the last 3 years of business and inviting them to another Grand Extravaganzas, and that was a "Customer Appreciation" party. Which was created to enhance the Customer <u>Connection/Relationship</u> for the "Retain and Refer Process" to prosper for continuous growth and success!

Eventually waterbeds lost their grip hold on the marketplace, and get this, "Sun Valley Water Beds" eventually became "Mor" Furniture and I moved on to radio and learned the <u>process</u> of... **"Branding the Brain"** on the other side of the coin as well as another format in communications.

Now let's do some **'Referral Math'**, and see how much <u>more</u> business can be earned…

Let's say YOU earn 15 Consumers (**off the market**), now Customers in a 1-month period of time, and YOU receive 2 referrals each, that is 30 referrals. At an average of 30% that are actually interested equates to 9 **"Legitimate Referrals"**. And if YOU recall of the statistics I gave earlier, there is a 75% chance of taking these Consumers (Referrals) off the market. Which are pretty good odds! Where a fresh walk-in will be taken off the market at a 25% closing ratio. So, by continuing what has been instructed so far in this Process of Improving (<u>Betterment</u>) a process, I would calculate that YOU would be able to double that 25% closing ratio. Equating to a 50% closing ratio of which those referrals will be earned, equating to an average of 4 to 5 more earned Customers within that 1-month time period. If you're selling cars that's pretty substantial!

Bottom line…<u>" Referrals" Pay Off!!!</u>
SPREAD THE WORD… "<u>YOU</u>"!!!

The "Betterment Process"
Of Doing "What's Right"

Epilogue

There are 3 **purposes** for this *"Betterment Process"* that was generated with *"Motivated "Passion"* to initiate a conducive tutorial that would be of **assistance** to enhance, and or strengthen any process that may already be incorporated into any Company's protocol, and not to be intended to demean any One individual's process, but again to enhance it!

In our society it is well known the difference between *"Right"* and wrong, and unfortunately a reminder is sometimes in check (*safety inspection*), or simply a directed reminder. Because it's already in YOU! But unfortunately there's another misfortune, and that is some actually need to be directed in doing **"What's Right"**; Second **purpose** for this tutorial! Third **purpose** and Bottom line…is so that *"Customer Relationships"* can be spawned and *"Retained"* with *"Referrals"!*

There is absolutely nothing wrong with being directed as long as "One" knows that they need to be directed. This indicates that a *"Betterment Process"* becomes a prerequisite in One's strive for success! And there is absolutely nothing wrong with that either, but quite the contrary. As they now say… "kudos" to YOU!!!

"Betterment" '*is an act (*action*), or process of **improving** something'; 'a making or **becoming better**'*!

What has been devised in this *"Betterment Process"* of doing *"What's Right"* include 3 of the 6 instrumental ingredients to *"Inevitable Success"*, and that is *"Structure", "Process", and "Management",* which is direction! The other 3 ingredients are entirely up to "YOU" … *"Passion", "Motivation" and "Action".*

Like any food dish or gourmet meal, to come out successful where it's harmony to the pallet and has a craving for more, it requires ALL the required ingredients as well as following the proper directions. So, ensure that YOU incorporate <u>all</u> the required ingredients with no shortcuts, and YOU will have them saying…

"*My compliments to the chef*"!

Final directive and question… Will YOU be doing things by **"Choice"** or by **"Chance"**? Think about it…

www.ingramcontent.com/pod-product-compliance
Lightning Source LLC
LaVergne TN
LVHW061035070526
838201LV00073B/5045